'This text will make even the most reluctant "poet" fall in love with poetry. Readers will be inspired by the "power of poetry to transform lives" and as a result will be motivated to explore teaching poetry not only in English lessons but across the curriculum, whilst enjoying doing so! This book will give you the confidence to be creative and likely create your own classroom poet's appreciation society!'

Catherine Carden, Staff Tutor, The Open University

'Bower writes with a gentle authority that nurtures confidence and inspiration in teachers who are keen to give poetry a place in the lives of their pupils. Bower's mission in this exciting new book, is to reveal the truth, beauty and imagination that comes from poems. She does this well because of the combination of her own love of poetry and a thorough, practical knowledge of the realities of modern classroom life.'

Andrew Lambirth, Professor of Education (Literacy), Faculty of Education and Health, University of Greenwich

POETRY AND THE 3-11 CURRICULUM

Poetry can enable learners to engage, learn and have fun, whatever their cognitive, linguistic or social levels and this book provides a great many examples of how this might be achieved. This exciting and innovative text provides a wide range of ideas for using poetry to enhance the early years and primary curricula, and therefore the learning experience of all children. Each chapter contains ideas for pedagogy and practice, underpinned by research and classroom experience ensuring that practitioners will come away feeling much more confident to teach this genre and better enjoy poetry themselves.

Throughout, there are discussions around specific pedagogies and practices relating to the use of poetry across the curriculum, as well as resources – including a wide range of poems from diverse countries and cultures and poems in different languages – and activities which can immediately be used in the classroom. Ideas are provided in terms of how poems can be employed in different subject areas, to introduce or reinforce concepts, engage children in more challenging concepts, ensure that lessons are fun and engaging and develop children's awareness of other people and places beyond their immediate experience.

This book is an extremely powerful combination of informed discussion – drawing on ideas from different theoretical perspectives including recent findings from neuroscience – and practical suggestions for every classroom. Armed with this text, practitioners will not only have a very strong idea of how to use poetry to enhance their curriculum but also why this is such a compelling genre.

Virginia Bower has been involved with different aspects of education all her life. Starting as a self-employed businesswoman, she moved into primary school teaching and leadership, before moving to higher education and teacher training. Her interests are in primary English, poetry and supporting children with English as an additional language.

POETRY AND THE 3-11 CURRICULUM

Enhancing the Learning Experience

Virginia Bower

LONDON AND NEW YORK

Cover image: © Getty Images

First published 2023
by Routledge
4 Park Square, Milton Park, Abingdon, Oxon OX14 4RN

and by Routledge
605 Third Avenue, New York, NY 10158

Routledge is an imprint of the Taylor & Francis Group, an informa business

© 2023 Virginia Bower

The right of Virginia Bower to be identified as author of this work has been asserted in accordance with sections 77 and 78 of the Copyright, Designs and Patents Act 1988.

All rights reserved. No part of this book may be reprinted or reproduced or utilised in any form or by any electronic, mechanical, or other means, now known or hereafter invented, including photocopying and recording, or in any information storage or retrieval system, without permission in writing from the publishers.

Trademark notice: Product or corporate names may be trademarks or registered trademarks, and are used only for identification and explanation without intent to infringe.

British Library Cataloguing-in-Publication Data
A catalogue record for this book is available from the British Library

Library of Congress Cataloging-in-Publication Data
Names: Bower, Virginia, author.
Title: Poetry and the 3-11 curriculum : enhancing the
learning experience / Virginia Bower.
Description: Abingdon, Oxon ; New York, NY : Routledge, 2023. |
Includes bibliographical references and index.
Identifiers: LCCN 2022022374 | ISBN 9780367722753 (hardback) |
ISBN 9780367722791 (paperback) | ISBN 9781003154174 (ebook)
Subjects: LCSH: Poetry-Study and teaching (Primary)-Great Britain. |
Poetry-Study and teaching (Early childhood)-Great Britain. | Language arts
(Primary)-Great Britain. | Language arts (Early childhood)-Great Britain.
Classification: LCC LB1527 .B68 2023 | DDC 372.640941-dc23/eng/20220810
LC record available at https://lccn.loc.gov/2022022374

ISBN: 978-0-367-72275-3 (hbk)
ISBN: 978-0-367-72279-1 (pbk)
ISBN: 978-1-003-15417-4 (ebk)

DOI: 10.4324/9781003154174

Typeset in Interstate
by Newgen Publishing UK

This book is dedicated to Peter who proofreads, comments and keeps me going.

And to Mum and Dad – thanks for all the poems.

Family reading time
The author's partner's grandchildren enjoying sharing a rhyming storybook

CONTENTS

	Introduction	1
1	The power of poetry	11
2	Poetry to develop speaking and listening skills	22
3	Using poetry to develop decoding and comprehension skills	34
4	Promoting an enjoyment of writing through poetry	46
5	The power of poetry to promote a multicultural, multilingual approach	58
6	Using poems in science and maths	69
7	Poems for times and spaces	84
8	Poetry in the digital age	97
9	Getting creative with poetry	109
10	Poetry for physical and mental health and wellbeing	121
	Index	134

Introduction

A personal beginning...

My enduring memories of poetry emerge from my mum reading to me every night from *The Oxford Book of Children's Verse* (Opie and Opie, 1973). The rhythms and cadences of those poems have stayed with me through my life and appear in my mind at unexpected moments. As I am cycling around English country lanes or through Portuguese orange groves and I see a cat, giving me its defiant stare in the way only cats can, words from T. S. Eliot's 'Macavity the Mystery Cat' ping into my mind, the prosody of this poem, firmly imprinted in my memory.

Equally, Blake's very different feline poem struck a chord with me from a very young age, with its chant-like rhythm and hypnotic cadence:

> Tyger Tyger, burning bright,
> In the forests of the night;
> What immortal hand or eye,
> Could frame thy fearful symmetry?

At the age my mother read this poem to me, I would have had no inkling as to the meaning of words such as 'immortal' or 'symmetry'; and of course, no idea of the symbolic meaning attributed to both this poem and Blake's 'The Lamb'. All I knew (albeit unconsciously) is that this nightly reading represented routine, safety, security and love and these feelings still rise to the surface when I return to the verses locked into my brain. I remember the delight of waiting for the final lines of Christina Rossetti's poem, 'What is Pink?':

> What is orange? Why, an orange,
> Just an orange!

These lines never lost their power to ignite a spark of joy, and the evocation of sights and sounds and smells in this delightful poem are to be treasured. I am conscious at this juncture, however, of the need to acknowledge two important points. First, my experience is not everybody's experience, and may well not be yours, and there will be children you teach who have never had poetry read to them or had the chance to explore it for themselves (although unconsciously they are often engaging with it in the form of playground games, nursery

DOI: 10.4324/9781003154174-1

rhymes etc.). Second, even if one's childhood included exposure to poems, it is important to remember that what one experiences as a child and therefore falls back on when teaching (whatever the subject or genre), is *limited* and *limiting* and that, as with any discipline – the arts, science, mathematics – ideas and approaches move on. The poems we might enjoy as a child may not appeal to the children we teach two decades later and we need to be ready to learn from our pupils and open our minds to new poetic worlds.

I have no doubt that my experience of poetry from a very young age contributed to my love of words, books, word play, different languages, teaching English (particularly poetry) and reading and writing poems throughout my life. We are all made up from the experiences, feelings, beliefs, information we encounter through our lives; the people we meet, the places we go, our hopes and aspirations, our disappointments and dashed dreams, failures and triumphs. For me, poems have contributed to what makes 'me' and I am grateful for this. I believe this underpins my desire to champion poetry in early years and primary settings whenever possible; to give children a tile that will be a small part of the mosaic that is their lives. A tile that can never do harm; only good. A tile that we are not always overtly aware of, and yet, if removed, would – indeed, should – leave a gaping hole in our mosaic.

What can poetry offer?

I would argue that the purpose of education should be to promote a love of learning and an understanding of how we learn and to inspire curiosity about and respect for the world in which we live (Bower, 2020). This holds particularly in relation to nature, the environment, sustainable development, enduring friendships, empathy and understanding and an appreciation of both local and global matters. Poetry has the potential to allow for this approach to education, particularly in relation to the easy access to thousands of poems on just about every subject you can imagine. For those who take more of a human capital stance to education, whereby school is seen as preparation for a working life in order that a healthy contribution to the economy is possible, the argument for poetry still stands. Hennessy and Mannix McNamara point out that 'innovation rather than standardisation' (2011, p. 19) is what employers require and the opportunities for innovation within discussions around poems and poetry writing are unlimited. Through poems, learners hear the voices of others and can allow their own voice to be heard – important facets of most jobs and careers. Not only that but, perhaps more importantly, poetry delivers 'segments of beauty, valuable pieces of truth, and flashes of imagination' (Alghadeer, 2014, p. 87) and what more can we aspire to in our approach to language and literacy than beauty, truth and imagination?

We live in challenging times and children are exposed to concepts through multiple media, often before they can understand the meaning or import of these. This can cause anxiety and uncertainty, and often young people are left to try to make sense of what they see and hear. Poetry can help with this sense-making. In poems, children hear the echoes of their own concerns, in the words of others. They can articulate their own thoughts and questions through creating their own poems – a free and freeing outlet for feelings and emotions. Beyond the more serious themes found in poetry, there are also clever, funny, witty, life-affirming poems which can allow children to laugh, play with words and let their own creative juices run riot!

More prosaically, the latest Ofsted framework (DfE, 2019) reignites a focus upon a broad and balanced curriculum for young children, 'introducing them to the best that has been thought and said and helping to engender an appreciation of human creativity and achievement'. The framework also advocates a focus on personal development – resilience, confidence, independence – and the importance of young learners discovering what they are interested in and developing these interests and talents. Again, poetry has the power to provide high quality examples of what humans can be and create, and the wide-ranging subject matter of poems enables children and teachers to explore their own interests and be innovative with their own approach to poetry. As well as this, the breadth of poems across the ages allows us to question what is 'the best that has been thought and said' and to appreciate that this is something that should not be dictated by those that hold power; rather, children and teachers should be given the opportunity to decide what appeals and speaks to them.

If, for whatever reason, a canon of texts is suggested and/or imposed, there are considerable and potentially damaging effects in terms of what texts are included and the relevance of these texts to our 'superdiverse' (Vertovec, 2007) population. This imposition also restricts exposure to a breadth of poetry because of lack of curriculum time. Cremin et al. (2008, p. 456), put forward that, although having a deep and extensive knowledge of particular authors is not to be disregarded, 'breadth and diversity' are essential to give children a valuable and exciting reading experience.

The challenges

Poetry is a much-undervalued genre and its place within the early years and primary curricula is often marginalised, giving way to approaches to literacy which are deemed more straightforward to teach and assess and have more perceived 'value' in economic terms. Hennessy and Mannix McNamara (2011) found, in their research, that consumerism, results, performance and so on all dominated the perceptions of pupils (post-primary) and their teachers because of the pressure of exam results and levels of accountability. The pupils in this fascinating study could see no alignment between studying poetry as a genre in its own right and studying poetry for the exam. One of the pupils said 'I like to focus on improving my college chances rather than increasing my knowledge base' (ibid., p. 214). They could see no point in studying poetry for its own sake and only 6.5 per cent of the pupils surveyed felt that the genre was an important part of the course: 'For such pupils, meaningful engagement with poetry equated with exam preparation and assimilation of pre-scripted responses' (ibid., p. 211). Although this research was undertaken with post-primary pupils, there is considerable significance to be acknowledged for those of us teaching in early years and primary settings. Embedding an enjoyment of and interest in poetry from an early age may well be the catalyst for secondary pupils to approach their experiences of poetry in later years in a more positive way. Early exploration of a range of poetic forms might provide a starting point from which they do not simply see the study of poems as the necessary evil for passing an assessment, but as something that is already part of their unique mosaic.

In terms of genre, poetry in early years and primary is often the underdog, giving way to narrative and non-fiction with which teachers are generally more comfortable. A report into the teaching of poetry in schools (Ofsted, 2007) found that, of all the aspects of the English curriculum, the teaching of poetry was the weakest, with a very limited range of poems utilised, many of which did not challenge the learners to any degree. I strongly believe that we cannot put the blame on teachers for this. Because of testing, accountability, reporting of results and so forth, overwhelming priority is given to core subjects (English of course being one of these) and, within these subjects, particular areas – currently, phonics, spelling, grammar. Teachers face a recurring tension between wanting to be culturally responsive and plan a curriculum that is relevant to the children and acknowledges their experiences, backgrounds and interests, whilst being told what to teach and how to teach it (Dymoke, 2012).

Although poetry can enhance learning in all these areas, it is not seen as the priority medium and there are very few opportunities for professional development in this area. In Initial Teacher Education, poetry often comes in as the poor relation in terms of coverage, as the time in university – to explore, share, discuss, read and write poems and better to understand the theory and research behind the pedagogy and practice – is ever-shortened (indeed, many school-based routes into teaching will have zero hours allotted to this).

Teachers may lack confidence with the planning and teaching of poetry and have themselves often had adverse experiences in their own education where they have been asked to read poems aloud or write poems with very little guidance; or worse still, have had to analyse poems until the genre loses all appeal. Cremin's (2013, p. 23) research indicated that teachers' knowledge and confidence relating to poetry was weak, with nearly a quarter of those involved with the study being unable to name one poet. In her chapter which focuses on the emerging identity of a poetry teacher, Cremin points out that teachers' reading identities inevitably impact on opportunities presented to children and, when we think of it like this, it is clear why poetry is rarely a primary classroom priority. What we choose, as teachers, to read, enjoy, share and discuss has a strong influence on what children choose to read, enjoy, share and discuss and if poetry is not on our agendas, it is unlikely to appear on children's, unless there is a strong interest at home.

From my many and varied conversations over the years – with experienced and trainee teachers – I have come to realise that many avoid teaching poetry, and often come with 'poetry baggage' (which does not seem to happen quite as much with prose). Maybe they have had negative experiences of poetry in school and their memories of this can deter them from exploring poetry with children, beyond what they judge to be absolutely necessary. In their research, Hughes and Dymoke (2011, p. 49) found that teachers' opinions fell into different categories:

- Poetry is boring
- Poetry is elitist
- Poetry needs to be relevant
- Poetry is 'frill', on the periphery
- Poetry is too difficult to evaluate/assess
- Teaching poetry tends to just focus on analysis
- Poetry is a solitary art

If we look briefly at each of these in turn, we begin to realise the impact this might have on children's experience of poetry in their formative years of education. The first two opinions – poetry is boring/elitist – are likely to emerge from teachers' own encounters with poetry in school. Perhaps poems were introduced which were far removed from their life experiences and which seemed to belong to another time and place – restricted to those 'in the know'. This links to the third point, focusing on the importance of relevance to the pupils we teach. This can be challenging in terms of curriculum time, our own breadth of knowledge to enable us to choose poems that will resonate with our young learners, and the pressure to teach a particular poetry canon. The next opinion which emerged from Hughes' and Dymoke's research – that poetry is 'frill' – demonstrates how often our own experience of a subject or topic or genre influences how we approach it with others. If the teaching of poetry is just something to tick off once a term, or a luxury that there is little time for, rather than being embedded in everyday practice, it will indeed be perceived as 'frill'. I hope that, through this book, I will 'prove' that poetry is far from just 'frill'!

The next point – that poetry is challenging to evaluate and assess – is undoubtedly something that concerns most teachers – whatever phase they work in. Dymoke, Lambirth and Wilson (2013, p. 103) found that the English subject lead teachers in their study highlighted three key issues with assessment of children's poems. First, the assessment tools provided in each setting were mainly designed for prose and if you are trying to 'tick off' aspects of learning, using provided criteria, poetry does not 'fit'. Linked with this, they felt that teachers needed knowledge for assessment – what to assess. They questioned whether we need criteria or whether this genre is too personal to assess. The third issue identified links with this personal aspect and they put forward the ideas that poetry is untouchable and individual; that poems come from children's hearts and that, if we are going to assess them, we need a very sensitive approach to advising on crafting and editing. It was felt that, often, teachers have neither the confidence nor understanding of poetry to do this. However, one of the teachers in the study seemed to find an effective balance as she 'combined a determination to make interventions into the development of children as writers of poetry in school alongside the recognition of the sanctity and uniqueness of the children's private individual work' (ibid., p. 108).

If we return to Hughes' and Dymoke's list of opinions from teachers, the penultimate is around the fact that poetry teaching tends to focus on analysis. This may be particularly the stance of secondary phase teachers, who are under pressure to develop pupils' analytical skills. In early years and primary, there is not the need for this focus, but of course, poems are wonderful resources to improve comprehension skills, and sensitive approaches to this, which do not remove the pleasure of just listening to or reading poems, can be very powerful (see further discussion of this in Chapter 3).

The final point – that poetry is a solitary art – finds its foundations, I would argue, in an idealised portrayal of poets, sitting in privileged solitude, isolated from the hustle and encumbrances of everyday life, writing alone and often leading bohemian existences! Even without this image, it is true that often writing is a solitary occupation – whether it be creating fiction, writing newspaper columns or putting together an encyclopaedia. However, what leads up to this writing is rarely solitary. It often requires interviews, visits to libraries and archives, discussion with friends, family, experts, a sharing of opinions, perspectives and ideas and a gathering of information from a vast range of sources. In other words, it is collaborative, even if the drafting, editing and production of a final piece takes place in a more isolated state. All of this collaborative work is highly appropriate for young learners as they engage in research, conversations, sharing and exploring. How the written piece is approached is of course down to the management of the classroom but putting the notion of poetry as a solitary art to one side will be beneficial to all.

The points made by the teachers that emerged in the Hughes and Dymoke study are invaluable because they raise questions and bring to the forefront teachers' concerns, allowing us to confront them and, to some extent, put them to bed. If we do not confront our demons and continue to marginalise this genre, young children are deprived of the chance to build a love of poetry and bring to the classroom what they already know and enjoy about poems. Harmer (2000, p. 15) writes that 'poetry is as natural a process for primary children as swimming, running, breathing or eating chips' because of the rhymes, songs, raps, jingles, song lyrics, advertisements and so forth, they encounter from the moment they are born. If we fail to capitalise on this knowledge and experience, opportunities will be lost in terms of developing children's effective use of language and an awareness of the power of words alongside a better understanding of themselves and their place in the world. Poetry has the potential to achieve all this and more.

Aims of the book

This book aims to address many of the challenges mentioned above and to highlight the power of poetry to enhance all areas of the early years and primary curricula and to improve the school experience more generally for all children through the sheer enjoyment of poetry. In a relatively recent project undertaken by the Centre for Literacy in Primary Education (CLPE) (2017), involving workshops for 20 teachers run by a tutor and poets, the following findings emerged:

- The need to give poetry a more prominent place in the curriculum;
- The power of poetry in terms of finding one's own identity and exploring the identity of others;
- The importance of hearing poetry read aloud and having the chance to practise and perform poems;
- The value of opportunities to read poetry for pleasure, without the need for a response and having the chance to then respond and reflect, not just analyse;
- The benefits of teachers being readers of this genre and having the opportunity to discuss their responses;
- The need for professional development opportunities for teachers in this area of the curriculum, including working with poets so that they can find their own writing voice.

This book responds to these findings, explicitly and implicitly including ideas – theoretical and practical – to support the use of poetry across the curriculum. Drawing on key research from this relatively 'niche' field, each chapter provides an evidence-informed rationale for the use of poetry to support learning and promote children's interest and motivation. The first chapter begins by discussing why poetry is such a powerful genre when used in a flexible, innovative way, emphasising the idea that, although poetry is a powerful way of supporting language development and highlighting literary devices, this should not be to the detriment of just enjoying the genre for its own sake. Through poetry we can understand more about ourselves, others, the world around us and our place in the world. The chapters then move into more specific focuses – speaking and listening, reading and writing – before ranging out across curriculum areas and subjects. Although this structure might appear to 'silo' aspects of the curriculum, this is not the intention. Rather, it is hoped that the reader can dip into chapters to gain ideas for upcoming teaching or to plan ahead and use the chapter headings to guide with this, whilst also engaging with the whole book as an interconnected web of ideas, where disciplines converge and become stronger through the common theme of poetry.

I have deliberately included poems, links to poems and the names of poets at every opportunity; the intention being that, even if you do not go beyond the pages of this book in terms of developing poetry pedagogies in your setting, you will have a wealth of examples to read, use and enjoy. Sometimes, where poems are out of copyright or if they are my own examples, I have been able to include the whole text or part of it. Where this is not permitted, I have provided a link so that you can access the poem yourself. The chapters include reference to poems from a range of countries and cultures, including poems in different languages. Ideas are provided in terms of how poems can be employed in different subject areas, to introduce or reinforce concepts, engage children in more challenging concepts, ensure that lessons are relevant and engaging and develop children's awareness of other people and places beyond their immediate experience. Each chapter contains three or four examples of activities you can use or adapt for the children in your class. These are not aimed at specific year groups or age phases; rather it is hoped that you can examine the activities and decide which are most suitable for the children you teach or which can be modified – either by resource or pedagogy – to be a better fit.

There are times in schools when it seems that curriculum coverage, driven by the pressure of assessments and the resulting accountability, takes much of the pleasure out of learning and teaching. Any resources, pedagogies, strategies and activities which can bring life and energy into the classroom are to be valued and this book argues that poetry – in its myriad forms – has the potential to achieve this.

Chapters

Chapter 1: The power of poetry

This first chapter argues that poetry has the potential to transform lives; opening up worlds to young learners that might not be accessible in other ways. It begins with the pragmatics of using poetry, illustrating how easily accessible this genre is for busy practitioners. The chapter then goes on to explore the power of poetry and provides ideas about when you might use this genre across the curriculum. The idea of developing a positive pedagogy and connecting curriculum are linked with poetry, before examining how poetry can be used to promote language awareness. Children finding a voice through poetry is another theme of this chapter, before a final section focuses on the benefits of poetry throughout our lives. As with all the chapters, there are practical ideas to finish.

Chapter 2: Poetry to develop speaking and listening skills

There are three key sections in this chapter: using poetry to develop speaking skills; using poetry to develop listening skills; and practical activities for the classroom. Within the speaking section, themes focus on rote learning, learning by heart, recitation and performing, before exploring how poetry might enhance questioning, debating and discussion. The listening section considers how listening to others reading poems can enhance children's experience and their learning, and then examines how listening to others' responses to poems is also of great value.

Chapter 3: Using poetry to develop decoding and comprehension skills

This chapter argues that the reading curriculum and reading across the curriculum can be brought alive for children through poetry. Promoting an enjoyment of reading and the ability to read critically are partly our responsibility as practitioners and poetry has the power to do both. Arguments are offered which present the idea that teaching children to decode text can involve far more than standardised discrete phonics lessons and that poems contain all the necessary resources to support children as they continue their reading journey. In the same way, this genre has everything you need to develop young learners' comprehension skills and practical ideas are provided for both these aspects of reading.

Chapter 4: Promoting an enjoyment of writing through poetry

Chapter 4 begins by examining why it is that poetry writing might inspire more/better writing generally, before moving on to explore two key themes relating to the teaching and learning of poetry writing – the advantages and challenges of using models and the advantages and challenges of writing freedom. The chapter concludes with four examples of activities you might use to promote an enjoyment of poetry writing and therefore – hopefully – writing more generally.

Chapter 5: The power of poetry to promote a multicultural, multilingual approach

This chapter begins with a focus on making connections between poetry and languages, highlighting how poetry can be the ideal resource for drawing attention to language – whether this be the linguistic diversity of our pupils or the foreign language we have decided on for curriculum coverage. Within this section there are specific suggestions for the use of collocation, lexical sets and cognates. The chapter then moves on to exploring how we might use poems in different languages, to promote and celebrate linguistic diversity, before doing the same for a celebration of different cultures. The chapter ends with three activities to set you off on your journey towards a poetry-inspired, multilingual, multicultural classroom!

Chapter 6: Using poems in science and maths

This chapter puts forward the idea that poetry can be used to enhance the science and maths curricula or, in the case of the early years curriculum, the areas relating to these subjects. The importance of linking disciplines to promote a creative approach is discussed with reference to three particular elements: utility, originality and aesthetics. The chapter then examines specific examples of how poetry might be used to enhance science-related teaching and learning, including a focus on metaphor, before exploring the use of poetry within maths. The maths section examines three themes – counting, constraints and patterns.

Chapter 7: Poems for times and spaces

The key focus of this chapter is how poetry can enable a better understanding of the world in which we live – past, present and future – with the early years curriculum held up as an exemplar. There is a section focusing on how significant issues, with an historical or geographical focus, might be explored by poetry. This is followed by a discussion relating to the use of poetry to learn about people and events in history, and then a geography focus suggesting how geographic enquiry might be enhanced through poems.

Chapter 8: Poetry in the digital age

One of the key aims of this chapter is to think about how we might use poetry to make the curriculum more accessible for children and how digital tools might support this. The chapter begins by examining how poetry 'fits' with digital learning and provides some examples of potential connections. The main section focuses on multimodality and how the modern, digital world allows children to innovate, experiment and explore, bringing their existing knowledge and understanding to classroom tasks, and transforming the learning experience. As with all the other chapters, there are practical suggestions for the classroom to finish.

Chapter 9: Getting creative with poetry

In this chapter, there is a focus on the arts – more specifically painting, song, dance and drama – and how poetry might be used (as an art form in its own right) in conjunction with these, to enhance children's experience. The chapter includes a practical classroom activity for each of these art forms, with examples of how poems can be used in a range of ways.

Chapter 10: Poetry for physical and mental health and wellbeing

We would all like to think that children's physical and mental health are at the forefront of decision making in school – whether this be to do with curriculum, pedagogy or assessment. However, in an age of accountability, surveillance and the questioning of our professional judgements and decisions, this is not always straightforward. This chapter provides ideas on how poetry can be embedded in everyday practice to support children's – and indeed our own – physical and mental health. Health is a vast topic and I have therefore chosen, in the first section of this chapter, to look specifically at physical *activity* and the connections between physical activity and learning, and how poetry can become an effective part of this. This includes a focus on embodied cognition. I then move on to examine the ways in which poetry can support children's (and our own) positive mental health and wellbeing, bringing in examples of powerful poems that might be utilised.

References

Alghadeer, H. A. (2014) 'Digital Landscapes: Rethinking Poetry Interpretation in Multimodal Texts', *Journal of Arts and Humanities*, 2, 87-96.

Bower, V. (2020) (ed.) *Debates in Primary Education*, Abingdon: Routledge.

CLPE (2017) *Evaluation of the Centre for Literacy in Primary Education (CLPE) Power of Poetry Training Programme*, London: CLPE.

Cremin, T. (2013) 'Exploring Teachers' Positions and Practices', in Dymoke, S., Lambirth, A. & Wilson, A. (eds.), *Making Poetry Matter International Research on Poetry Pedagogy*, London: Bloomsbury, 22-33.

Cremin, T., Mottram, M., Bearne, E. & Goodwin, P. (2008) 'Exploring Teachers' Knowledge of Children's Literature', *Cambridge Journal of Education*, 38, 4, 449-464.

Department for Education (DfE) (2019) *Education Inspection Framework*, London: DfE.

Dymoke, S. (2012) 'Opportunities or Constraints? Where Is the Space for Culturally Responsive Poetry Teaching Within High-stakes Testing Regimes at 16+ in Aotearoa New Zealand and England?', *English Teaching: Practice and Critique*, 11, 4, 19-35.

Dymoke, S., Lambirth, A. & Wilson, A. (eds.) (2013) *Making Poetry Matter International Research on Poetry Pedagogy*, London: Bloomsbury.

Harmer, D. (2000) 'Poetry in the Primary School', *Education 3-13*, 28, 2, 15-18.

Hennessy, J. & Mannix McNamara, P. (2011) 'Packaging Poetry? Pupils' Perspectives of Their Learning Experience Within the Post-primary Poetry Classroom', *English in Education*, 45, 3, 206-223.

Hughes, J. & Dymoke, S. (2011) '"Wiki-Ed Poetry": Transforming Preservice Teachers' Preconceptions About Poetry and Poetry Teaching', *Journal of Adolescent & Adult Literacy*, 55, 1, 46-56.

Ofsted (2007) *Poetry in Schools: A Survey of Practice*, London: Ofsted.

Opie, I. & Opie, P. (eds.) (1973) *The Oxford Book of Children's Verse*, Oxford: Clarendon Press.

Vertovec, S. (2007) 'Super-diversity and Its Implications', *Ethnic and Racial Studies*, 30, 6, 1024-1054.

1 The power of poetry

This first chapter argues that poetry has the potential to transform lives; opening up worlds to young learners that might not be accessible in other ways. It begins with the pragmatics of using poetry, illustrating how easily accessible this genre is for busy practitioners. The chapter then goes on to explore the power of poetry and provides ideas about when you might use this genre across the curriculum. The idea of developing a positive pedagogy and connecting curriculum are linked with poetry, before examining how poetry can be used to promote language awareness. Children finding a voice through poetry is another theme of this chapter, before a final section focuses on the benefits of poetry throughout our lives. As with all the chapters, there are practical ideas to finish.

Introduction

With most things in life, if we can see a good reason for doing or exploring or studying something, the more motivated we are. The relevance, the significance, the influence – these all must be understood and rationalised to ensure that we consider something is worth the time invested. If these are not secure, it is likely that other options take our attention and become the priority and those deemed less essential make their way to the bottom of the priority list. This is where we often find poetry in educational settings.

In this chapter, I will argue that poetry has the power to transform lives – quite a strong assertion you might think, but one to which I am totally committed. This transformation can simply be through sharing poems with the children you teach – enjoying the emotions they invoke, the way they offer new perspectives on the world, the voices they represent. I am a huge advocate of simply appreciating this magnificent art form and ensuring that we create poetry 'bubbles' (Lambirth, 2021, p. 262) where, in the safety of their classrooms, the teacher and the taught can shrug off the culture of accountability and age-related targets and immerse themselves in worlds created by the words of others. However, this book intends to go beyond poetry for poetry's sake and to examine the power poetry has to transform the curriculum, with a more deliberate and systematic approach to the integration of this genre across the early years and primary school day. This should never supersede the reading and writing of poetry for the sheer love of the genre, but I would argue that, if we can bring it more to the attention through curriculum areas, we leave further doors open for our children to seek out this genre because they know of and appreciate its existence. Poetry is powerful material, too important to leave to chance and too useful to be ignored.

The chapter begins by considering some practical aspects of using poetry across the curriculum. I start with this because, to best utilise the power of poetry to enhance teaching and learning, we need to know how to access resources easily and in a timely manner. The chapter then moves on to examine how and when we might consider incorporating poetry into our school days, with examples of linking with learning objectives from the early years and primary curricula. The idea of positive pedagogies and a connecting curriculum are then explored, and how poetry fits into this, before moving on to the power of poetry to enhance language awareness and to support children with finding their own voice. The final section, before the practical activities, discusses the power of poetry beyond the classroom and how it can have a lifelong impact. As with all the chapters, I finish with some activities that I hope you can take straight back into your settings and enjoy with the children!

Pragmatics

This might seem a strange place to start when discussing the power of poetry, but I would argue that, as practitioners, we are always having to take a pragmatic approach in terms of how much time we can devote to a subject or theme or topic; what resources we have available; what evidence do we need to provide about each child's progress, and so forth. Poetry, therefore, can be one of your most powerful resources because poems rarely cost anything, are very easily accessed and on the whole take very little time to read. There are wonderful poetry anthologies, and I would certainly recommend asking for a small budget in school, to allow you to purchase a range for your book corner.

Be an agent of change and go to your headteacher to ask for this finance. Try to go with a clear argument as to why poetry is a powerful resource and how you intend to use poems, both in your own class and across the school. For example, I would regularly take assemblies and read poems to the whole school, perhaps on a theme that all pupils were addressing, for example climate change. Most headteachers, if presented with a clear rationale, will at least listen to your case if well argued. Harmer (2000, p. 16), writes that, 'poetry is not expensive. The most important resource is a commitment from the headteacher' and this is what you need to seek. If funding is not available, there are anthologies at very low costs, which you might want to purchase yourself. With these in your toolkit, you can share at least one poem every day with your class. That is 190 poems over the course of a school year! This means 190 opportunities for children to listen, share, laugh, discuss and think and probably taking an average of five minutes a day. Here are some reasonably priced, useful anthologies:

A Poet for Every Day of the Year by Allie Esiri
Now We Are Six by A.A. Milne
Street Child by Taiwo Oluwakayode and Samantha Beardon
On the Move: Poems About Migration by Michael Rosen and Quentin Blake
101 Poems for Children Chosen by Carol Ann Duffy: A Laureate's Choice by Carol Ann Duffy and Emily Gravett

Even without anthologies, you can easily share a poem a day by accessing poetry websites. Here are some examples, which I refer to often throughout this book:

> The Children's Poetry Archive https://childrens.poetryarchive.org/
> The Poetry Zone https://poetryzone.co.uk/
> Poetry4kids www.poetry4kids.com/
> Poetry Foundation www.poetryfoundation.org/learn/children
> Michael Rosen www.michaelrosen.co.uk/

So, you have the resources – step 1√. It is then important to plan the reading of poems into each and every day (and maybe homework/holiday reading also). Having a set time is probably best, as it is not then 'bounced' from the timetable because you are running late. Ten to nine was always a favourite time for me, after the register but before assembly or the first lesson of the day. I had the anthology, 'A Poem for Every Day of the Year' and this was my starting point. If I did not have time for any others, I would always read the day's poem. I would also try to link this to each child's birthday, and I would say for example, 'This poem is for us all, but most especially it is for Barnaby, as it is his special day!'

Sometimes children would be keen to read the poem of the day for me (always to be encouraged where possible). At other times, I would have it on the board ready for when they arrived in the morning so that they could access it themselves (dependent on age group of course). If I had a little extra time, I would give each group a copy of a poem/different poems and encourage them to read together, discuss and then perhaps do a choral reading (see Chapter 2 for a discussion about the power of choral reading). There are myriad ways to bring poetry into your classroom, requiring very little time or effort, and the powerful effect of this inclusion will soon be felt as you notice children's vocabulary growing and their ideas expanding. Often, children start to lead the initiative themselves; bringing in poems they have found or written, choosing poems for you to read or reminding you that you have not yet read the poem of the day! These are good signs that poetry is becoming embedded in your classroom ethos.

Recognising the power of poetry and when to use it

Although it is quite enough to just weave poetry in the ways described above into your daily routine in a fairly random way (by this I mean, with no specific focus or theme), there are approaches to make this an even more powerful experience, of benefit to you and your pupils. For example, instead of an arbitrary poem selection, you could have a theme for the week/month/term – the weather, for example – which might link with other subject areas. In the Early Years Foundation Stage guidance, Development Matters (DfE, 2021), you can find the following objectives:

- Explore and respond to different natural phenomena in their setting and on trips.
- Begin to understand the need to respect and care for the natural environment and all living things.
- Recognise some similarities and differences between life in this country and life in other countries.
- Understand the effect of changing seasons on the natural world around them.

If weather is your theme – and there are so many poems on this topic – then you could easily be addressing some of these objectives through poetry (see Activity 1 below and more discussion about using poetry in geography-related sessions in Chapter 7). You could perhaps start or finish a carpet session with a poem, play audio versions of poems to emphasise a key point or ask children to join in with a song, rhyme or verse which focuses on the weather and seasons. There is a superb collection to get you started on the Poetry Archive for Children site – https://childrens.poetryarchive.org/collections/wonderful-winter/ – entitled 'Wonderful Weather', with audio versions (plus transcripts) by a range of poets.

In Key Stage 1, the National Curriculum Programme of Study for Geography states that children should:

- Identify seasonal and daily weather patterns in the United Kingdom and the location of hot and cold areas of the world in relation to the Equator and the North and South Poles.

and in Key Stage 2:

- Describe and understand key aspects of physical geography, including: climate zones, biomes and vegetation belts, rivers, mountains, volcanoes and earthquakes, and the water cycle.

There are plenty of poems suitable for these age groups relating to weather, climate, geographical areas and features – you would not be in short supply – and they are another way of introducing a concept/topic and of ensuring that poetry is integrated across all curriculum subjects. I have given weather and climate as an example here, but there are poems to be found on just about anything, so keep an open mind! Once you start thinking of poems as a resource and having some at hand when you plan across the curriculum, you will begin turning to them more regularly and with confidence. Your bank of poems will soon grow and, instead of having to search for relevant examples, you will have them sitting there in your collection. Try to involve children in this, so that they are bringing poems to share with you and their peers, and their voices are heard through the poems they choose. Through these opportunities, choices and multiple voices, a pedagogy of possibility and positivity will emerge, through the medium of poetry. The next section examines this idea of positive pedagogy in more detail.

Positive pedagogy, poetry and a connecting curriculum

Jonathan Barnes has written for many years about 'positive pedagogy' and encapsulates the essence of this in the following quote: 'Positive pedagogy depends on well-articulated aims and fulfilled teachers in settings where emotional, physical, sensory and intellectual connections are constructive' (Barnes, 2018, p. 18). He goes on to emphasise the importance of being 'human and humane' in all our dealings with children and colleagues, which stems from self-awareness (acknowledging our strengths and aspects we find more challenging), and an ongoing focus on ensuring environments that reflect our values. This includes the resources used, the way we talk to each other, the promotion of empathy, celebration of difference and a willingness to make connections – with people, places, objects, feelings – even if this takes us away from planned objectives.

Barnes writes about these links within his concept of the 'connecting curriculum'. By this he does not simply mean connections within and between curriculum subjects. This is certainly part of it (and much of Barnes' work focuses on cross-curricular approaches and interdisciplinarity), but he also emphasises the importance of teachers connecting with their pupils in highly personal and innovative ways. In a project wherein Barnes and colleagues observed tutors working with trainee teachers (Grainger, Barnes and Scoffham, 2004), effective connecting strategies included the use of humour and anecdotes, opportunities for collaboration and reflection and responding to student responses in an open and friendly way. This enabled the students to make more effective and authentic connections between subjects and their own existing experiences and knowledge; as well as creating strong, connected relationships between student and student, and students and tutor.

So, how does poetry fit into this idea of a connecting curriculum based on positive pedagogy? Poetry is usually written because the poet has a strong message they wish to convey. This might be humorous, tragic, angry, soulful – whatever the emotion or feeling or subject matter, a great deal of the writer is invested in the words and structure of the poem. Often, the poet is sharing their beliefs and 'putting themselves out there' to make connections with their readers, or indeed, with their inner selves. The result – if a connection is successfully made with a reader – is a shared experience, maybe because the reader can immediately make associations with their own life or a place they have visited or a situation they have encountered.

It might be that the rhythm, cadence and prosody of the poem connect the reader to a physical or mental experience. An example of this might be Robert Louis Stephenson's 'From a Railway Carriage', where we can feel the rhythm and movement of the train:

> Faster than fairies, faster than witches,
> Bridges and houses, hedges and ditches;
> And charging along like troops in a battle,
> All through the meadows the horses and cattle:
> All of the sights of the hill and the plain
> Fly as thick as driving rain;
> And ever again, in the wink of an eye,
> Painted stations whistle by…

Similarly, Auden's 'Night Mail' evokes the rhythms of the train, and the atmosphere of the journey. A clip from the film with the poem being read is available here: www.youtube.com/watch?v=zmciuKsBOiO

It might be that connections are made with personal experiences – those moments when we read something and think, 'That is just how I felt!' or 'What memories that brings back!' A lovely example of this is Valerie Bloom's 'Granny Is' which evokes the sights, sounds and smells of a person and a place. This person and this place might be very familiar to our young learners, or very different to anyone/anything they have encountered. Either way, the poet brings powerful images to connect us to 'Granny'. You can find this poem here: https://childrens.poetryarchive.org/poem/granny-is/.

Joan Poulson's 'Pictures in My Mind' is another wonderful example that allows us to connect to home and the wider world – https://childrens.poetryarchive.org/poem/pictures-in-my-mind/. There will be children in our classes who have travelled widely and can bring their experiences into school and share; they will recognise certain aspects of this poem. There will be others who have not travelled beyond their local space, and who might not relate to the 'sky that's blue as hyacinths' and 'water bright as rainbows'. However, pictures can form in their minds about the wider world and what might await them; powerful words insinuating themselves into their thoughts, bringing a warm, colourful glow. If this 'exotic' landscape is beyond imagining for some, Poulson also evokes the joy of the familiarity and comfort of home; the place one knows the best, for better or worse. These are the poems children need to hear, share and discuss. It is here that positive pedagogy and creating connections can have the transformative impact we would wish for in all our teaching and learning transactions.

Promoting language awareness

I would argue that poetry can draw our attention to the myriad ways language can work to produce an emotion, to inform, to make us think about the world in different ways. The concern however is that, if we over-analyse and potentially impose our own meaning onto a poem, drawing attention perhaps to particular use of language, then we are ignoring what children bring to each poem and their own interpretations. Simecek and Ellis (2017, p. 98) focus on this, when they examine the uses of poetry and their concern is that, if we utilise poems solely to draw attention to structure, form, vocabulary and so on (an instrumental approach), then we are in danger of 'missing the importance of poetry as poetry and the rich aesthetic experience it affords'. There is a balance to be achieved here, because, to *not* use poetry to draw attention to language in practice is a missed opportunity; but to see a poem simply as a way to tick off an objective or to make a didactic teaching point is to lose the essence of the genre itself and its potential to meet 'a deeply human need' (ibid., p. 99).

One way to ensure this balance is always to provide space for children to read, re-read, discuss, question and respond to poetry. Even if we are just reading a short poem to start the day, there is nothing to stop children returning to this poem during the day or taking the poem home to revisit or share. This should be encouraged, particularly if you do not have the intention of spending more time on a particular poem. This is about developing a culture and ethos within your classroom, which reflects a belief that reading is both an individual and a shared experience. Promoting the idea that what each and every one of us brings to a poem or a piece of prose and what we then take from it will be very different and that this is fine – in fact it is brilliant, exciting, to be celebrated! Wilson (2021, p. 80), writes that 'until a reader engages with a poem, igniting it with a combination of her interest and experience, the text will lie "dormant"', and this is a lovely way to approach poems with young learners. You can emphasise that the poem is 'sleeping' until the reader's engagement awakens it to become what they want it to be, through an awareness of the language used.

This culture and ethos can be promoted and developed through showing an awareness and enjoyment of different genres and media; modelling responses and demonstrating an interest in how words and images are presented and portrayed. Poetry is just one reading resource here of course, but its unique power lies in the gap between what the words mean and how they are interpreted. Within this gap we can 'dwell in possibilities' (Simecek and Ellis, 2017, p. 105) and this perhaps gives us an idea of the quality of a poem – 'we can start to see how the use of language in exemplary or paradigmatic works of poetry offers a heightened and more complex twofoldness of communicative content than can be found in ordinary language use' (ibid.).

Have a think about how you might 'dwell in possibilities' with this haiku by Kobayashi Issa (1763–1828), one of the most famous Japanese haiku poets:

> Everything I touch
> with tenderness, alas,
> pricks like a bramble.

The use of language here is beautiful and seems to encapsulate the feeling we can have at times when whatever we attempt seems to end unsatisfactorily. However hard one tries, things are not turning out the way we want. Most of us will have experienced this feeling at one time or another, and we know we need to move beyond this to keep persevering and achieving our goals. What a great way to introduce this to children, provoking an awareness of the language used by Issa to create this effect and discussing their own feelings in these situations.

Language in poetry can often allow us insights more difficult to attain in other genres. Feelings can be implied, leaving the reader to find their own meanings from the language used. Some poems 'speak' to us more than others and if we can normalise the use of poems across our school day, there is the likelihood that all children in your class will begin to find language that speaks to them and that they might adopt in their own oral and written utterances. The next section focuses on this a little more.

Finding a voice

Language awareness is inextricably linked with children finding their own voice; something to be promoted whenever possible. UNICEF and Save the Children (2011) produced a resource guide entitled, 'Every Child's Right to be Heard' and the guide highlights how giving children a voice, encouraging participation and listening to children is so important. I have adapted some of their points here to illustrate the impact of empowering children to find their voice:

- Contributes to personal development;
- Promotes better decision-making;
- Protects children as they feel confident to speak up for themselves;
- Prepares children to become flourishing and active members of society;
- Provokes an awareness of difference and diversity;
- Develops an accountability for their ideas and actions.

In a project organised by the Centre for Literacy in Primary Education (CLPE) (2017), where teachers engaged with poetry workshops, one of the teachers reflected on how few opportunities were given to children to find their own voices. Enabling children to find their voice should, I believe, be firmly embedded in our pedagogies across the curriculum subjects, and poems provide the ideal vehicle to express thoughts and feelings, discuss subjects of interest and make links with voices across the globe. In her blog for National Poetry Day 2019, Charlotte Hacking writes that, 'Poetry is the ultimate form of creative expression; children can have complete control of what they want to write about and how they choose to best express their ideas' (Hacking, 2019), and this choice and control gives them a voice they might not normally feel empowered to discover and use. You can read some of the poems that Charlotte includes in her blog, written by children of different ages here: https://clpe.org.uk/blog/finding-voice-through-poetry-blog-national-poetry-day.

Exposure to a wide range of poems enables children to hear writers express themselves in hugely different ways. In turn, this provides the realisation that they too can have a voice of their own and can find new and exciting ways to express ideas, whether this be through choice of vocabulary, length of lines, poetic form and so on. Sometimes it can be difficult for us to find a voice in different settings and situations. These feelings are reflected in many poems and can be a way for children to recognise that finding a voice, an identity, is not easy. There is a powerful poem here – www.chabad.org/theJewishWoman/article_cdo/aid/447548/jewish/Who-Am-I.htm – entitled 'Who Am I?' which might be a useful example to use with older children. However, even with very young children it is good to explore the notion of voice and identity and you can find a whole range of poems on this subject here – https://childrens.poetryarchive.org/collections/who-am-i/.

Going beyond the classroom

This final section examines the power of poetry in terms of its impact beyond school. Promoting poetry throughout the early years and primary education, so that children go into secondary schooling with a positive attitude towards this genre, is vital and, as educators, we have a responsibility to ensure this. However, there is a far longer reach in terms of lifelong learning and instilling an interest in poetry which offers mental health benefits into our more advanced years. Not only this, but poetry has the power to connect different generations, to cross cultural and linguistic boundaries and to build networks whereby a shared language forges bonds and relationships.

I wanted to finish this chapter with an example of the power of poetry to connect with a group of people for whom life is extremely challenging: people with dementia, their carers and families. The reason I have chosen this goes back to my words at the very start of the chapter; that for most of us, having a very strong reason for taking an approach in life provides the motivation to tackle and sustain that approach, despite challenges. Surely there can be no more powerful reason than to feel we can be doing something constructive for all those – and this may indeed be ourselves – who are affected by dementia. I could replace 'dementia' with any number of other mental and physical benefits for different medical conditions, and this exemplar will, I hope, simply provide the catalyst for your own thought processes and conversations.

Gregory's (2011) article focusing on how poetry can be used to improve the quality of life for people with dementia (PWD), reports on a project entitled, 'Try to Remember'. The findings of this project included an awareness that poetry could enable PWD to explore and preserve memories; that poetry could improve communication between PWD and their carers and families; and that the creating and sharing of poetry and ensuing conversations had the effect of 're/humanizing dementia sufferers in the eyes of those who care for them' (ibid., p. 160). As part of the project, a poet sat with PWD and asked them to reminisce and talk about anything they wished. The poet recorded their words, verbatim, took them away and turned them into poems, using the original words as much as possible. These poems were then read aloud in individual or group sessions (sometimes including families as well as carers), and copies were kept in patients' records.

Many of the reminiscences were about day-to-day life decades ago, rather than generic 'typical' themes which the older generation tend often to be encouraged to talk about – World War 2, for example. These everyday life memories made them considerably more personal and individual and often families heard stories about their relatives' lives which they had never been aware of. The carers also learnt more about the experiences and life histories of their patients, providing them with topics to discuss with PWD whilst engaging with the more mundane caring tasks. A wonderful quote from Gregory states that 'Care staff argued that clients' memories were captured in the poems, pinned like butterflies before their colours faded' (ibid., p. 165) and, during the read aloud sessions, PWD who may not normally have been responsive to outside stimuli, recognised and responded when they heard their own words revealed through the poems. Gregory concluded that, because poetry very often relates to the social and emotional, it might be one of the best placed of the arts in terms of supporting PWD and their carers, and improving the 'sense of self, mood, confidence, cognitive functioning, behaviour and quality of life' as well as the environment in which the PWD is residing.

This is just one example within one isolated project and article, linking mental health and poetry. However, it can be from these small seeds of information that interest, awareness and action arise and if it can provide yet more justification for promoting poetry at every opportunity, and perhaps exploring and conducting research with other groups of people, so much the better.

Activities

Activity 1: Poems around themes

Linking poems to themes and topics and objectives across the curriculum enables you to approach learning in different and powerful ways. Instead of starting a lesson with questions or a video or finding out what the children already know, you could start with a poem. For example, if your chosen theme was the weather, you could start with Ken Nesbitt's poem, 'This Winter I Went Sledding' – www.poetry4kids.com/poems/this-winter-i-went-sledding/. Earlier in the chapter, one of the Early Years Foundation Stage objectives was 'To understand the effect of changing seasons on the natural world around them'. After a reading of this poem, a discussion could be had about snow and its impact on us and on the natural world. This could lead to ideas about animals hibernating, birds migrating, plants and flowers becoming dormant. These concepts are challenging but children will always surprise us with their existing knowledge – often gained from television programmes or websites – and are more than capable of reflecting on important concepts such as climate change, impact on seasons and so on.

What starts out as a one-minute reading of a light-hearted poem, can lead to conversations that promote a depth of learning about global issues. There would also be the opportunity to explore another objective: 'Recognise some similarities and differences between life in this country and life in other countries'. Children could share examples of when they have played in the snow or have seen this in television programmes from other countries. Which countries are more likely to have snow? Why is this? Would you like to live there?

Activity 2: Acting the part!

This activity brings poetry and acting together and offers children the chance to bring their own interpretations and voice to a poem. You can use any poem suitable for the age group you teach. I have chosen 'Adventures of Isabel' by Ogden Nash – https://allpoetry.com/Adventures-Of-Isabel – and the activity is quite challenging and more suitable for older children. However, if you were to use a nursery rhyme or poem appropriate for younger learners, you could also simplify the activity.

Explain to the children that they are going to change a poem into a four-act play. The chosen poem has four stanzas and is full of action and excitement so should make an excellent performance.

Read 'Adventures of Isabel' by Ogden Nash and ensure the children have a copy each so that they can follow the poem as you read. Discuss the four stanzas. Re-read the poem and then ask the children to retell it as a story (this will familiarise them with the key incidents and the vocabulary). You could do this by going round the class and inviting individuals to contribute a sentence. Anybody who does not want to can just pass (having the choice is important).

By this time, the children should have a very good knowledge of the poem. Divide them into groups and ask each group to choose a stanza that they would like to change into a scene for a play (if there are arguments, you will have to draw lots!). Explain that they can use the words from the poem if they wish, or they can make up their own dialogue – it is up to them – but the main theme of each stanza should remain the same.

Give children time to prepare and practise their scene (this might go over several lessons) and then use a large space – preferably the hall or a stage – to perform the poem as a play. If possible, record the performance so that you can use it to compare with the original poem and have some time to discuss how the children have used their own voice to create their version.

Activity 3: Writing from experience

Earlier in the chapter I discussed the importance of giving children the opportunity to find their own voice, and poetry is ideal for this, particularly if we relate it to children's own lives. Start by choosing a subject that you know will engage the children in your class. This could be linked with a topic you are studying or if you do this activity just after a break from school it might be linked with what they did on holiday. If possible, the subject needs to be relevant to all the children, so that they are able to draw on their own experiences – these might be physical experiences such as losing a tooth or their morning routine.

For the purposes of this example, I am going to use a trip to the seaside as the subject matter. Ask children if they have ever been to the seaside and if they remember their first trip to the seaside. Give them some time to discuss with a partner and then share ideas with the whole class. Read 'At the Seaside' by Robert Louis Stevenson:

> When I was down beside the sea
> A wooden spade they gave to me
> To dig the sandy shore.
> My holes were empty like a cup.
> In every hole the sea came up
> Till it could come no more.

Do they remember digging holes and making sandcastles? Discuss the children's memories and experiences.

Write out Stevenson's poems as prose in two sentences – modelling on the board. This will show the children that to create a poem, they only need to think of two ideas, put them into sentences and then think about how they will present them on the page in poem format. Change the prose back into a poem, showing where the line breaks work.

If there is time, the children can write two sentences about their experience at the seaside and then change this into a poem.

References

Barnes, J. (2018) *Applying Cross-Curricular Approaches Creatively*, Oxon: Taylor & Francis.
CLPE (2017) *Evaluation of the Centre for Literacy in Primary Education (CLPE) Power of Poetry Training Programme*, London: CLPE.
Department for Education (2021) *Development Matters*, London: DfE.
Grainger, T., Barnes, J. & Scoffham, S. (2004) 'A Creative Cocktail: Creative Teaching in ITE', *Journal of Education in Teaching* (JET), 30, 3, 243-253.
Gregory, H. (2011) 'Using Poetry to Improve the Quality of Life and Care for People with Dementia: A Qualitative Analysis of the Try to Remember Programme', *Arts and Health*, 3, 2, 160-172.
Hacking, C. (2019) *Finding a Voice Through Poetry*. Available at: https://clpe.org.uk/blog/finding-voice-through-poetry-blog-national-poetry-day. Accessed on 14.01.2022.
Harmer, D. (2000) 'Poetry in the Primary School', *Education 3-13*, 28, 2, 15-18.
Lambirth, A. (2021) 'Teaching Poetry Within an Accountability Culture', in Bower, V. (ed.), *Debates in Primary Education*, Abingdon: Routledge, 254-266.
Simecek, K. & Ellis, V. (2017) 'The Uses of Poetry: Renewing an Educational Understanding of a Language Art', *Journal of Aesthetic Education*, 51, 1, 98-114.
UNICEF & Save the Children (2011) *Every Child's Right to be Heard*, London: Save the Children.
Wilson, A. (2021) 'The Reader, the Text, the Poem: The Influence and Challenge of Louise Rosenblatt', *Education 3-13*, 49, 1, 79-95.

2 Poetry to develop speaking and listening skills

There are three key sections in this chapter: using poetry to develop speaking skills; using poetry to develop listening skills; and practical activities for the classroom. Within the speaking section, themes focus on rote learning, learning by heart, recitation and performing, before exploring how poetry might enhance questioning, debating and discussion. The listening section considers how listening to others reading poems can enhance children's experience and their learning, and then examines how listening to others' responses to poems is also of great value.

Introduction

At a time when the purpose of education is often questioned and debated – in terms of preparing children for an uncertain and, arguably, unimaginable future – it is important to remember that some skills are fundamental, whatever the future holds. I would suggest that two such skills are speaking – fluently, confidently and in a range of settings and situations – and listening – 'real' listening which involves identifying what lies on the surface of what is heard as well as learning how to achieve the finer nuances of reading below the surface and between the lines. Listening which prompts a response to what the speaker has said, as opposed to merely responding with something that *we* want to say (something of a bugbear of mine and which I will explore further later in the chapter!).

To my mind, poetry allows for – indeed ensures that – these complex skills develop, sometimes through overt pedagogical approaches but, more often, through the intrinsic absorption of what poems have to offer and the responses they evoke. Opportunities to explore new and vibrant vocabulary and to try out these unfamiliar words in oral and written form are unbounded with this genre because there are poems on anything and everything! Poems can lead the way into conversations about people, places, events, emotions, experiences, fantasies and realities. They are the perfect conduit for discussion and debate as every poem is open to individual interpretation and it can be a significant moment for children when they realise their opinion and ideas are as valid as anybody else's. This can provide a voice – where, theretofore, confidence may be lacking – and a lexicon with which to articulate thoughts and ideas.

This chapter is divided into three key parts, with sub-sections within each. First, the idea of using poetry to develop speaking skills is explored with an initial focus on rote learning,

learning by heart, recitation and performing. I then go on to examine how poetry can enhance questioning, debating and discussion skills. The second main section has a focus on poetry to develop listening skills, starting by considering the power of listening to others reading poems aloud before moving on to thinking about how listening to the responses of others – to poems – is of great value. The chapter finishes, as do all the chapters, with practical activities to use in your classroom.

Using poetry to develop speaking skills

This section examines two approaches to this genre which, although very different, demonstrate the power of poetry to develop useful and empowering speaking skills. The first explores the idea of rote learning, learning by heart, recitation and performing poems and the second discusses how poetry can be used to develop questioning, discussing and debating skills and promote a confidence in expressing personal viewpoints.

Rote learning, learning by heart, recitation and performing

The most obvious example of developing oral skills, if we are thinking about articulation, enunciation and pronunciation, is the recitation of poetry. This is often associated with rote learning and, for some of us perhaps, bad memories of having to 'perform' to an audience. This 'bad press' has been, in the last decade, exacerbated by the views and actions of a previous education secretary – Gove – who pushed for greater focus on rote learning, poetry and recitation in the revised National Curriculum (DfE, 2013) – harking back, it seemed, to times long past. It is a pity that divisive politics often muddy the waters of genuine debate which can more usefully – and in a robust way – examine the potential advantages of promoting such skills as memorisation and recitation, as well as recognise the challenges. I will examine some of these now.

A good starting point is to consider Andrew Motion's ideas (cited in Cliff Hodges, 2016), who argues that rote learning and learning by heart are not the same. Rote learning tends to be for a very specific purpose and can be undertaken with very little thought relating to the content being committed to memory. Learning by heart, on the other hand, is to be deeply engaged with the experiences that poems put forward and remembering them because of the beauty encapsulated in the way the poem is presented and because they 'talk' to us. This idea is expanded by Bailey (2016, p. 393), who writes that, 'When we know the words by heart, their associated images seem to cut loose and take on a life of their own.' This deep engagement with poetry is in stark contrast to the somewhat mechanistic requirement of rote learning, merely for the sake of being able to repeat information. That is not to say of course that rote learning does not have a place in the early years and primary classroom; but, with poetry, learning by heart seems more appropriate to a genre which speaks to our hearts and minds, as individuals.

Evidence suggests that the impact of learning poems by heart is considerable and enduring. Pullinger and Whitley (2016) undertook research to find out the poems people remembered; when, where, how and by whom poetry is learned; and how people feel about memorising and reciting poems. One of their underlying questions related to whether *memorising* poems triggers understanding that differs from that achieved by simply reading poems or analysing them. Their findings at the time (the project was still ongoing) led them to identify three emerging themes: 'the living poem', 'the indwelling poem' and 'the loved poem'. The living poem emerged from participant responses in terms of how poems relate to them and how this might change over time, with connections made in relation to a person or a place, a time in life or other literary experiences. The poem, of course, stays the same; but we change and so therefore does the impact of the poem. However, its unchanging nature provides a rock in the shifting waters of our lives.

The second theme involved what they termed an 'indwelling poem' which in some way reveals a relationship between a poem and our bodies and senses. The authors provide specific examples of this, such as how a line might be the length of a breath or 'the unit length of working memory'. Here we can start to see how the memorising of lines of poetry has direct links with cognitive functions, emotions and feelings and the development of deeper thinking: 'Memorised, the poem opens up dimensions of space and time within the mind' (ibid., p. 319).

The 'loved poem' is the third theme emerging from the research and relates to the *feeling* we have for a poem rather than what emerges from analysis. Over 90 per cent of the responses to open-ended questions in Pullinger and Whitley's research included the word 'love' and the authors ask the question whether our emphases on determining the meaning of poems – even in primary settings – 'tend towards substituting analysis over feeling' (ibid., p. 320) in an attempt to gain meaning.

Often, as classroom practitioners, we are required – through top-down directives – to teach and assess in ways that may not accord with our values or principles. This is inevitable as we live and work in an age of surveillance and accountability and, if we are not vigilant, this can become demoralising and demotivating. To avoid this, keeping hold of what should be our main priorities when working alongside children – ensuring learning is engaging, relevant and varied (in content and mode of delivery) – allows us to keep hold of a sense of ourselves and to feel that we are doing the very best for our pupils. Poetry is a way of ensuring this, as it has the potential to reach those children for whom learning may be challenging. We surely want to hear children saying how much they love a poem and hear them quoting lines from those they have read or listened to? You can see from Pullinger and Whitley's findings how powerful and enduring an experience this can be.

Bayley (2016), in his paper focusing on poetry, memory and the unconscious, goes so far as to say that poetry literally saved him. Having been written off by his teachers – he describes himself at age ten as 'an almost complete educational failure' (ibid., p. 387) – Bayley found comfort and meaning in poems and memorising poems. He went on to win recitation competitions and, with the support of more understanding teachers and mentors, became a teacher and a psychoanalyst. Bayley's metaphorical depiction of poetry is powerful and emphasises the potential of this genre:

> To possess in my own mind the exact words chosen by a poet is to have a small room in the house of my being that contains that most invaluable of human productions, poetry, the words given to us by a poet. Words with which I can look out from my room on to my past and on to the world around me.
>
> (Bayley, 2016, p. 394)

Learning poems by heart does not necessarily need to lead to a performance and can simply be for the pure pleasure of doing so and with the extremely useful benefit of a deeper understanding of oneself and the poem. However, having an audience in mind can further enhance the experience as, in reading or reciting aloud, the performer brings the poem into being, transforming marks on a page into something unique to the readers and listeners (Cliff Hodges, 2016). In this way, we are going far beyond the implied curriculum aims of merely being able to recite something from an identified canon; rather, the spoken word leads the audience towards a better understanding of aspects of life and less accessible concepts.

For Bayley, learning and reciting poems opened the doors to a life that might have stayed beyond his grasp. However, we need to take care that this type of activity does not put undue pressure on children. There will always be those – children and adults – who love to perform and are happy to be in the spotlight; and there are those for whom this is their worst nightmare! For the latter group, this does not mean that learning by heart and reciting needs to be 'out of bounds' – it is about setting up suitable activities and easing children into this practice through fun and engaging activities without unnecessary pressure. Lambirth, in his chapter focusing on performance poetry (Lambirth, cited in Bower, 2011), suggests starting with a saying which has a memorable rhythm to it – the example he gives is a West Indian phrase, 'Bam Ba Litty Bam Bam (p. 55) – and getting the children to play with this saying, feeling its rhythms and cadences and repeating it using different accents, or changing the volume, or reciting using a happy/sad tone and so on. They can do this in pairs or small groups or, indeed, the whole class can chant together. Confident individuals might want to contribute their own ideas in mini solo performances.

Playing with words and making words work for you is a significant aspect of poetry and, using this simple yet effective activity, children can begin to recognise what poems can offer, preparing them for more complex investigations as time goes on. Think of some phrases you might use – *Abracadabra* perhaps, or *supercalifragilisticexpialidocious* – and encourage children to offer their own examples; things they have heard on the television or in their computer games. Encourage them to think about how the meaning can change dependent on how something is spoken. For example, if you articulate *Abracadabra* in a slow mysterious way, it conjures up a different image to if you repeat it in a high pitched, excited tone. It is important to give time to exploring the effects and the impact on the listener.

You could introduce some tongue twisters to really challenge the children (there is a website with useful examples here – https://flintobox.com/blog/child-development/tongue-twisters-kids) – and they could create their own and challenge each other, perhaps reciting in different voices or accents, as Lambirth (cited in Bower, 2011) suggests. Playing with language makes us braver with language use – oral and written. We become more prepared to take risks, to invent words, to guess at the meanings of unknown words. Learning by heart, to recite to an audience, provides the opportunity to know a poem so well that articulation becomes more natural and instinctive. Children begin to realise that there is no point to a performance if the audience cannot hear or understand what is being recited, and this provides powerful motivation for improving communication skills.

Something you might want to introduce into your classroom is 'spoken word' poetry, often performed in 'poetry slams'. Spoken word poetry is, generally speaking, poetry that has been written to be performed orally, to an audience. Poetry slams are competitions where these poems are performed and judged by selected members of the audience, but, perhaps more importantly, allow for whole audience interaction and evaluation. The performer will often gesticulate, engage with the audience, change intonation, volume, pitch and so on, bringing in degrees of musicality. Poetry slams are open to anybody to perform their poem, about any subject. Usually, they must not exceed three minutes and props or musical instruments cannot be used. Performances can be individual or in groups. All of these 'rules' seem ideal in terms of the traits we want to develop in our young learners. Whether children wish to be performers or members of the audience, a poetry slam is interactive, inclusive, engaging and a great deal of fun!

Poetry to develop questioning, discussing and debating skills

Responding to the work of Louise Rosenblatt (1978), Wilson (2021) explores the idea of what we bring to a poem and our response. He emphasises the importance of having a 'fundamental pedagogical belief' (ibid., p. 87) that children have experiences, knowledge, opinions and perspectives gained outside of school and which they can bring and use and share in the classroom. One of the best ways to access these ideas is through opportunities for extended discussion; discussions which can occur between pupils, between pupils and teacher and between pupils/teacher and poem. Because poems are seen as more open to interpretation, there is more scope for conversations which allow for a range of perspectives and opinions.

In Green et al.'s project (2016), the researchers read either a short story or a poem or a newspaper article to groups of participants and then asked them to orally retell the text. The group who listened to the poem tended to use narratives to find a way to understand the poem – they took their experiences to the poem and brought the poem to their experiences – and they were more tentative in their retelling with a tendency to keep options open as to the poet's meaning. So much of the time in school, children feel they need to find the 'right' answer – what I call the 'guess what's in the teacher's head' syndrome – and, although there is at times a place for this, there is more of a need for dialogic talk, where children can make 'substantial and thoughtful contributions', where the teacher does not 'merely test understanding, but guides its development' (Mercer, 2003, p. 74).

To provide effective contexts for dialogic talk and to promote the asking – by us and the children – of open-ended questions, we need to have poems at our disposal which encourage this. 'The Jumblies' by Edward Lear is an example of a poem which is likely to raise questions and provoke discussion. Here is the first of the six stanzas:

> They went to sea in a Sieve, they did,
> In a Sieve they went to sea:
> In spite of all their friends could say,
> On a winter's morn, on a stormy day,
> In a Sieve they went to sea!
> And when the Sieve turned round and round,
> And every one cried, "You'll all be drowned!"
> They called aloud, "Our Sieve ain't big,
> But we don't care a button! We don't care a fig!

> In a Sieve we'll go to sea!"
> Far and few, far and few,
> Are the lands where the Jumblies live;
> Their heads are green, and their hands are blue,
> And they went to sea in a Sieve.

When sharing this poem with children, you might want to start by asking them what they make of this first verse. It is important not to put words into their mouths, so I would avoid referring to it as a 'nonsense' poem and, at this stage, would not share biographical details about Edward Lear. In this way, you are leaving the poem open to interpretation and it is interesting to see if the children ask questions which demonstrate an understanding of the nonsensical qualities of the poem. This discussion and debate are likely to be prolonged, as there is much to spark conversation, just in this first stanza. If the talk starts to dry up, you might want to interject with, 'Is there anything you might ask of the Jumblies or the poet?' or 'What is so strange about going to sea in a sieve?' Before reading more of the poem, children could discuss what they think the next stanza will reveal and each group could come up with a scenario to retell or act out. This poem lends itself beautifully to drama and role play and the children could perhaps produce a freeze frame to represent what they think is likely to occur as the poem moves on.

Starting with a poem such as this – fun, engaging, not too demanding – allows children to find their voice and gain confidence in expressing their opinions. With 'nonsense' verse, there can be no rights or wrongs and children can let their own imaginations run free. When they then move on to engage with more challenging poems, they are in a better position to contribute to discussion and debate and are well-practised in formulating questions. In Cliff Hodges' research (2016), where students prepared poems for choral reading, some of the participants found that the discussions in which they were involved made the poems clearer to them or raised a different viewpoint on meaning. Sometimes, what initially seemed clear and straightforward became more complicated in the process of sharing and discussing. And of course, if we give children these extended opportunities for discussion, the opposite might also be true – where the opaque becomes transparent.

Using poetry to develop listening skills

So, from speaking to listening (both, of course, inextricably linked). Again, this theme is divided into two approaches to developing listening skills. First, the focus is on listening to poems being read by different voices, giving children the opportunity to recognise that interpretations and performances are unique to the person reciting the poem and that different styles might appeal more than others. I feel very strongly that children should hear voices other than ours, as the class teacher. After all, they are in our classrooms six hours a day, five days a week and that can test anybody's patience! They also need to recognise that they too have their own voice which needs to be heard. The second approach focuses on listening to others' responses to poetry and learning to appreciate that opinions will vary and that everybody has a right to be heard.

Listening to poems being read by the original poets or by a teacher or a fellow pupil

Gordon (2008, p. 224) conducted a fascinating study focusing on the impact of listening to poems being read; what he describes as 'the potential impact of voiced poetry'. His research question was 'How do children respond to poetry they hear from recordings, and what are the implications for teaching?' and he found that children were very interested in the people behind the voices in terms of dialect, accent and cultural backgrounds. His findings implied that listening to poetry and having time to respond to what is heard enables children to examine and use words in ways personal to them – they are in control of their interpretation – and to make sense of their world through poems, rather than perhaps teachers imposing their understanding of a written poem and the inevitable and customary analysis that tends to accompany this. Gordon also found that the children's responses to the poems, in the way they listened, recalled and performed 'entails at some level empathy, a momentary embodiment of the voice (and hence identity) just heard' (ibid., p. 230).

Gordon believes that the act of listening to poetry as opposed to reading it, links with the dated but powerful statement in the HMI pamphlet 'Teaching Poetry in the Secondary School' (1987, p. 22), which draws attention to the importance of approaches taken to poetry in terms of 'the wide range of emotional possibilities each word possesses according to its context, its speaker, its association, or its history'.

We need to be aware, however, that listening to poems may not be a familiar or comfortable experience for our pupils. Cliff Hodges (2016) found that the teacher trainees in her research project demonstrated initial discomfort when listening to five poems being read, one after the after without recourse to a written version. However, this soon changed to interest and enjoyment, as each group learned and performed choral versions of one of the poems and they listened to each performance. In this way, they were becoming accustomed to different voices and the diverse ways a poem can be presented to an audience. Introducing children to these voices can be incredibly empowering, as they realise that their own voice can emerge in a style that suits them. The more voices children can hear, reciting their poems in different ways, the more confident they should become with their own engagement with this genre and with use of voice more generally. When you choose poems, read by poets, it is good to try to find different styles of reading – to appeal to the diversity in your class. Here are some examples of poets who have unique approaches and I have included the online link for each:

> Michael Rosen – www.michaelrosen.co.uk/hypnotiser/
> Chrissie Gittins – https://childrens.poetryarchive.org/poet/chrissie-gittins/
> Roger McGough – www.youtube.com/watch?v=byov5O5N6bc
> James Berry – https://childrens.poetryarchive.org/poet/james-berry/
> Valerie Bloom – https://childrens.poetryarchive.org/poet/valerie-bloom/

Being given the opportunity to listen to a range of voices allows for a deeper understanding of not only the poem but people, cultures, emotions and our own place in the world. As Gordon (2008, p. 227) suggests, 'listening to poetry is not a means to an end; rather, it is inherently valuable'.

Listening to responses to poems

At the start of this chapter, I mentioned the importance of 'real' listening and responding, where we absorb somebody's response to a stimulus, and respond in a way that encourages them to expand on this and share their thinking. This is opposed to listening and then responding in a way that merely reflects one's own related experiences. Let me give you an example to show my thinking.

In Activity 3 towards the end of the chapter, I use the following poem:

I Eat My Peas with Honey
I eat my peas with honey;
I've done it all my life.
It makes the peas taste funny,
But it keeps them on the knife.
(Anon.)

Now, envisage an ensuing group work session, where children are discussing the poem. One child might say, 'I really do not like honey because I had a horrible experience when I was young'. A typical response (from both children and adults) is to immediately respond with one's own experience: 'Me too! We had a pot of honey on the table outside in the summer and all the flies kept landing on it!' Now, there is nothing inherently wrong with this and indeed, this would be a useful anecdote to encourage discussion. However, I have a strong belief that, as well as developing greater depth of discussion, the world would be a much more empathetic, kind place if we first addressed the initial speaker's point, before leading with our own. For example, a response which would encourage Speaker 1 to divulge more information might be, 'Oh! What happened to you then, to make you feel like that?' This is likely to lead to an authentic recount, and it is through these small insights into life histories that we learn more about our fellow humans and ourselves. Bruner (2002, p. 22) writes about the importance of giving children opportunities to 'create meanings from school experience that they can relate to their lives' and suggests narrative 'as a mode of thought and as a vehicle of meaning making'. These narratives can often be provoked by a poetry stimulus, but children need to learn how to respond in such a way that others will share their narratives and then listen in turn to their peers. Time taken to model this is time well-invested.

The curricula for early years and primary emphasise the importance of the development of listening skills. Development Matters (DfE, 2021, p. 23) provides an 'observation checkpoint' at six months – 'does the baby respond to familiar voices…' – followed by numerous references to listening through the ages and stages and then, states that children in reception will need to 'Understand how to listen carefully and why listening is important' (ibid., p. 34). The statutory requirements for Years 1–6 (DfE, 2013, p. 7), state that pupils should be taught to, 'listen and respond appropriately to adults and their peers'. Despite this emphasis, what I think is sometimes missed is the way we need to explicitly *teach* these listening and responding skills and plan for contexts that promote skills in these areas. Poetry is the ideal resource for this, as I hope to have illustrated thus far in the chapter. As children engage with poetry to develop their listening and responding skills, you should notice that they become more open-minded and accepting of the views and opinions of others. They become aware that listening contributes to their own understanding and that this ability to listen enables their own learning to move forward. These skills go far beyond the requirements of the curricula and provide an underpinning for the development of strong, reciprocal relationships with family and friends, invaluable competences to take into careers and an open-mindedness which is essential in our fast-paced, ever-changing 21st-century life.

Bringing speaking and listening together

Poetry allows us to listen to voices from different times and places, and these voices share ideas, debate the simple and the complex, engage with the real and the imaginary and allow others an insight into their perspective of the world and beyond. In this way, whether enjoying poems alone or with others, we can be active participants in poetry 'conversations'. Blake (2015, p. 108) believes that 'If we *listen* to poetry, we have access to that conversation; if we also *speak* poetry, we start to join in' (my emphasis). Thus, that inextricable link between speaking and listening is forged and, through poetry, we gain access to our own and others' voices. Poems which themselves have a strong voice; where the poet seems to be talking to a specific person or indeed to the reader, can be particularly useful to engage children in these conversations. Here are some powerful examples you might want to use:

> *Mother to Son*, Langston Hughes
> www.poetryfoundation.org/poems/47559/mother-to-son
> *The General*, Siegfried Sassoon
> www.poetryfoundation.org/poems/57217/the-general-56d23a7de4d1c
> *Chocolate Cake*, Michael Rosen
> www.youtube.com/watch?v=bY7AyGRct-E
> *Life Doesn't Frighten Me*, Maya Angelou
> www.familyfriendpoems.com/poem/life-doesnt-frighten-me-by-maya-angelou

---

Activities

The activities below bring together the elements discussed in the preceding sections. Hopefully you will see how speaking and listening, learning by heart, recitation and developing a deeper understanding of language and its power, can be interlinked.

Activity 1: Voiced poetry

Locate websites which have poets reading their own poems aloud. Here are some examples:

> Children reciting at The Globe
> www.poetrybyheart.org.uk/performancegallery/7-plus/
> Michael Rosen performing his own poems about his family
> https://www.michaelrosen.co.uk/poems-and-stories-about-my-family/

Tony Mitton's audio versions of some of his poems
   https://childrens.poetryarchive.org/poet/tony-mitton/
Videos of Roger McGough reading his poetry on YouTube
   www.youtube.com/results?sp=mAEB&search_query=roger+mcgough

Choose four or five poems to play the children. They could be by the same poet or a range of poets. The examples above have poems suitable for all ages. Play your chosen poems at least twice (more if requested by the children) and then give the children extended group discussion time where they choose one or two to talk about (you could provide some guidance questions or sit with groups of younger children). With older children, ask them to choose one of the poems, in written format, to discuss, learn and prepare to perform (this might take more than one lesson). Each group performs their poem to the class, giving plenty of time to discuss key aspects afterwards, for example:

- How was this performance different to the performance given by the poet?
- What influences how we decide to perform a poem?

With younger children, ask them which poem they prefer – they could vote on this – and re-play it several times. Prepare a whole-class version, with individuals or groups learning a line each to recite. Discuss what is important about performing a poem, focusing on listening to each other, clear articulation and a focus on pitch, tone and volume.

Activity 2: Encouraging discussion and debate

Children need topics to discuss which promote strong feelings and encourage debate and discussion. Benjamin Zephaniah's 'Who's Who?' is a very useful example to spark this – https://benjaminzephaniah.com/rhymin/talking-turkeys-5/?doing_wp_cron=1633069137.5109689235687255859375

   Before sharing the poem, put a list on the board of examples of people in different roles, for example firefighter, athlete, rugby player, chef. Ask the children to either produce a brief, written description of the people who might be in these roles or to draw a picture. Tell them to put these descriptions/pictures to one side and you will come back to them. Read 'Who's Who' by Benjamin Zephaniah. What are the messages here? Go back to the children's descriptions/pictures.

- What do they tell us?
- Do we tend to have an image in our heads associated with people and their roles?
- How are different roles portrayed in the media?

I do not think children are ever too young to start thinking about these issues and, with very young children you could have a discussion around the jobs their parents have, what they want to be when they get older and so forth, ensuring that we emphasise the idea that we can be and do whatever we choose, with hard work and commitment. With older children, you could introduce the ideas of unconscious bias and the effects of this, and there is the opportunity here for linking to history, women's rights, Black Lives Matter and other universal, enduring themes.

You could then read the children my alternative version of Zephaniah's poem (or a version of your own):

I Used to Think
I used to think cleaners were women
I used to think soldiers were men
I used to think teachers were boring
Until I became one of them!
(Virginia Bower)

Children could have a go at writing a stanza of their own and then performing them to create a whole class poem. This, with the earlier discussion, brings both the dialogic talk and oral performance into one activity.

Activity 3: Learning by heart

Learning poems by heart is made easier if, at first, they are short and have a discernible rhythm and possibly rhyme. Add to this a little humour and the children will be with you all the way! This next activity has all these elements.

Either read the poem 'I Eat My Peas with Honey' to the class or ask a volunteer to do so.

I Eat My Peas with Honey
I eat my peas with honey;
I've done it all my life.
It makes the peas taste funny,
But it keeps them on the knife.
(Anon.)

Repeat, perhaps with other children or a group of children reading (preferably several times), so that the rhythm and rhyme is absorbed. Give the children time to discuss this strange concept – of eating a green vegetable with sweet honey. Ask them to consider what it is about honey that leads to the poet eating it with peas.

Discuss the rhyme scheme, perhaps noting that, although 'honey' and 'funny' sound the same, they look very different on the page (contextualising your phonics and spelling work). Ask children if they feel there is a rhythm to this poem. Clap the rhythm as a class.

Introduce the idea of 'rounds' – one group starts reciting the poem and then, once they have completed two lines, the next group starts the poem and so on. In this way, each group has to listen to what other groups are saying, at the same time as listening to the other members of their own group – quite a challenge!

With this activity, the children will have the advantage of reciting with others, which can develop confidence. They will encounter the poem so many times that it is likely they will have it memorised by the end of the session (hopefully you might hear them reciting it in the playground or role play corner), and they will be starting their poetry journey through life. From small acorns, giant oaks grow...!

References

Bayley, N. (2016) '"A Long-Legged Fly Upon the Stream": Poetry, Memory and the Unconscious', *Changing English*, 23, 4, 387-395.
Blake, J. (2015) 'Poetry, Listening and Learning', in Dymoke, S., Barrs, M., Lambirth, A. & Wilson, A. (eds.), *Making Poetry Happen Transforming the Poetry Classroom*, London: Bloomsbury, 107-113.
Bruner, J. (2002) 'Tenets to Understand Cultural Perspective on Learning', in Moon, B., Shelton-Mayes, A. & Hutchinson, S. (eds.), *Teaching, Learning and Curriculum in Secondary Schools*, London: RoutledgeFalmer, 10-24.
Cliff Hodges, G. (2016) 'Becoming Poetry Teachers: Studying Poems Through Choral Reading', *Changing English*, 23, 4, 375-386.
Department for Education (2013) *Key Stage 1 and 2 Programmes of Study*, London: DfE.
Department for Education (2021) *Development Matters*, London: DfE.
Gordon, J. (2008) 'True Soundings: The Findings of the 2007 OFSTED Report "Poetry in Schools" and Pupils' Responses to Poetry They Hear', *Changing English*, 15, 2, 223-233.
Green, A., Ellis, V. & Simecek, K. (2016) 'Actual Texts, Possible Meanings: The Uses of Poetry and the Subjunctification of Experience', *Changing English*, 23, 4, 351-362.
HMI (1987) *Teaching Poetry in the Secondary School*, London: HMSO.
Lambirth, A. (2011) 'Poetry is Slamming: Different Ways to Perform Poetry in Primary Schools', in Bower, V. (ed.), *Creative Ways to Teach Literacy*, London: Sage, 55-63.
Mercer, N. (2003) 'The Educational Value of "Dialogic Talk" in "Whole-class Dialogue"', in Qualifications and Assessment Authority, *New Perspectives on Spoken English in the Classroom*, London: QCA Publications.
Pullinger, D. & Whitley, D. (2016) 'Beyond Measure: The Value of the Memorised Poem', *Changing English Studies in Culture and Education*, 23, 4, 314-325.
Rosenblatt, L. (1978) *The Reader, the Text, the Poem: The Transactional Theory of the Literary Work*, Edwardsville, MI: Southern Illinois University Press.
Wilson, A. (2021) 'The Reader, the Text, the Poem: The Influence and Challenge of Louise Rosenblatt', *Education 3-13*, 49, 1, 79-95.

3 Using poetry to develop decoding and comprehension skills

This chapter argues that the reading curriculum and reading across the curriculum can be brought alive for children through poetry. Promoting an enjoyment of reading and the ability to read critically are partly our responsibility as practitioners and poetry has the power to do both. Arguments are offered which present the idea that teaching children to decode text can involve far more than standardised discrete phonics lessons and that poems contain all the necessary resources to support children as they continue their reading journey. In the same way, this genre has everything you need to develop young learners' comprehension skills and practical ideas are provided for both these aspects of reading.

Introduction

If you ask the question, 'In which lessons would you normally find poetry being taught?', most people are likely to say, 'English', and I would agree! It might seem odd therefore, to dedicate a chapter to reading, within a book about using poetry *across the curriculum*. I would argue, however, that although poetry is of course studied in early years settings and primary schools as part of literacy learning, because, apart from any other reason, it is included in both curricula, it is not necessarily used extensively to improve decoding and comprehension skills. All too often, in my hundreds of visits to education settings, I have seen phonics lessons where sounds are being taught out of context, as if anything to do with reading can ever be decontextualised if it is to make any real sense! More often than not, the objective sought in one of these sessions can more usefully be taught through poetry. Not only does this contextualise the learning, but it has the potential to energise young learners and engage them in active, problem-solving investigations, as they begin to identify sounds in the poems and rhymes that surround them. Learning to read should be a joyous process, which embeds an awareness of the sounds of language and the meaning that lies behind the sounds. Poetry can provide a significant way forward with this.

In the same way, comprehension skills are often taught through prose or non-fiction. Now these genres are of great importance – I would never contest this – but there is so much to be gained from using poetry to deepen children's understanding – of concepts, vocabulary, feelings, themselves – alongside the other key genres.

This chapter, therefore, examines the rationale for proposing a more coherent integration of poetry throughout the English reading curriculum, exposing children to a daily diet of poems, which might then be connected with other areas of the curriculum. I begin by exploring the place of poetry in developing decoding skills, before moving on to comprehension. I admit that this separation is a little unhelpful, as I am advocating that decoding and comprehension go hand in hand! However, addressing one at a time allows for specific examples to be included and you will hopefully see how the two aspects of reading can connect, through the use of poetry. The chapter finishes with practical activities you could implement with different year groups to support children's reading in a meaningful and enjoyable way.

The place of poetry in developing decoding skills

Decoding text is exactly what it says on the tin! We are taught from an early age (or indeed, with many children, they teach themselves) to decode by assigning a sound to a written letter or series of letters, then to combine these to create a word. We can then pronounce the word (although we may of course not understand what it means) and, eventually, decode a sentence. There are many ways we get to this point, and systematic phonics sessions in school are just one of these and, arguably, one of the least effective (Weale, 2022). I say this because I question any teaching and learning which is not contextualised and made relevant and real to children (and adults) and feel that, at a time when resources are so freely available online – resources that go far beyond the 'match the sound to the letter' games – it is not necessary to reduce the teaching of reading to 20-minute, uninspiring timeslots.

In whatever ways we try to 'jazz up' discrete phonics lessons, by using online games, mini whiteboards, flashcards and so forth, nothing can compare to the use of 'real' texts to bring reading alive; to put letters and words into context. I do understand the need to fit reading sessions into very busy school days, and that the government's desire to accelerate children's reading progress by putting phonics 'first and fast' (Ofsted, 2010) has led to a school approach which accedes to policy, but somewhere along the line common sense must prevail. If children do not learn that reading is a rewarding and enjoyable process, they will not choose to read and will never go beyond a technical, mechanistic approach to this skill.

Jackson (2018) writes that the monitoring, assessing and accountability attached to learning to read and, more specifically, to phonics has 'conceptually separated reading for meaning from the process of decoding words'. She refers to Walker et al.'s study (2014) which found that participants from schools were referring to the fact that they had to complete their phonics teaching before moving forward with teaching comprehension. I would say 'that way madness lies' (Shakespeare, King Lear) and we are in danger of turning children away from reading, because they lose interest before experiencing the pleasures that reading can bring.

The government's faith in intense phonics drilling to achieve better reading scores within international reading leagues (Austin, 2021) is misplaced and not underpinned by credible research. Robust studies indicate that what raises test scores is the embedding of opportunities to read for pleasure, with access to a wide range of texts (Krashen, 2018). There is no evidence to suggest that putting children into ability sets at the age of five and six for phonics – according to a recent study, 76 per cent of schools were doing this (Bradbury and Roberts-Holmes, 2017) – has any positive effect on their long-term reading skills. Indeed, research indicates that ability setting promotes inappropriate behaviour and fails to close the achievement gap (Henry, 2015). The Education Endowment Foundation (no date) write that,

> Within-class attainment grouping may also have an impact on wider outcomes such as confidence. Some studies from the broader evidence base conclude that grouping pupils on the basis of attainment may have longer term negative effects on the attitudes and engagement of low attaining pupils, for example, by discouraging the belief that their attainment can be improved through effort.

Implementing ability sets from an early age is potentially irretrievably damaging. Although not explicitly linked with this, I had a very eye-opening experience when I conducted a small-scale enquiry for my own Masters project, focusing on children's opinions on reading. I interviewed six pupils in my Year 6 class, who were deemed to be fluent readers. I was exploring children's ideas about how they thought they reached that fluency and their views on reading. All of the participants agreed that they were fluent, confident readers and that they had built this up over time, using a number of different strategies (none of them mentioned phonics). All six children said that they *never* read for pleasure and that it was seen as a skill to acquire – the box to be ticked – before moving on to other pursuits perceived to hold more interest or benefits. What had made them come to this conclusion? If this was the feeling of high ability readers, what might be the damage done to those who have more of a struggle to read and are constantly reminded of this as they move to their 'low ability' groups through the day? This experience really made me re-think reading and how to teach reading and I resolved to bring delight and excitement back to my reading classroom. Poetry was one way I did this.

So, how can poetry support children's decoding, whilst promoting reading for pleasure, comprehension skills and ensuring that children 'grow into readers' (Jackson, 2018)? In the following section, I am going to focus on my '3Ps' for motivating young readers and improving their decoding skills: Prediction, Participation and Performance.

Prediction

Despite proclamations from government sources to the contrary (DfEE, 2007), making predictions when decoding texts is a powerful strategy. Poetry – particularly rhyming poetry – is ideal for this, as children can have great fun guessing the end words of lines. This also allows you to focus on specific sounds (if you are under pressure to follow a scheme and a sequence), because you can choose poems/rhyming story books which include rhyming words containing suitable phonemes. There are several ways you can go about this. In a whole class session, you could explain to children that you are going to read them a poem, but you are going to miss out the final word of each line. You could either encourage them to write the word they think it is on their whiteboards (a useful way of bringing in encoding) or they could call out their ideas (can get very noisy – but fun!) or raise their hands and then share their idea. This poem is a good example you might use (also mentioned in Chapter 6 in relation to counting in Maths):

I Went Fishing

I went fishing
Took some bait.
Didn't go early,
Didn't go late.

Caught eight fishes
To put in my pail.
Seven were mackerel,
But the eighth was a whale.

The seven were easy
To put into the tin,
But that whale caused me trouble
Before I packed him in!

Took my catch home.
What did mother say?
'Get those eight fish out of here –
We're having steak today!'

(Anon.)

Here, the rhyme for each stanza comes in lines two and four and you can explain this to children and ask them to listen out for the sounds. This is a perfect poem for a focus on the long /a/ phoneme and the different ways this can be spelt – /ay/, /a-e/ (split digraph) and /ai/. You could simply encourage the children to predict the words and recognise why and how they are making these predictions, leading to a powerful discussion about what prediction is based on. Or you could go further with a spelling investigation and split the class into teams. Each team has a particular grapheme to investigate for example /ay/ or /eigh/ and they have to find as many words as they can containing that grapheme in 60 seconds. In this way (forgive the pun!), you can collect many words in a very short time and immerse children in fascinating discussions around the craziness of the English spelling system! They then realise that it is not their 'fault' when they spell words incorrectly – it is just about learning which is correct in particular situations. Reading and spelling become part of a fun game here rather than a right and wrong 'test'.

Here is another poem you might use:

Jack Hall

Jack Hall,
He is so small,
A mouse could eat him,
Hat and all.

(Anon.)

With this poem, you have three rhyming lines to play with and children would very soon learn the poem after a few readings, embedding the rhymes into their minds and recognising the regular spellings of the words. You could then perhaps show them a stanza you have written, in the same style:

Rosie Tweet
Rosie Tweet
Is so neat
The tidiest girl
In all her street.
(Virginia Bower)

Again, plenty you can do here with different spellings of the same sound – /ee/ and /ea/ – and you could perhaps put together another stanza as a class.

Participation

For many decades now, active learning has been promoted as a sound and effective approach, building on early theories around constructivism – learners building knowledge and understanding through adding to their existing experiences, often in a collaborative context. There is evidence to suggest that pedagogies that promote active learning and participation have the potential to reduce the achievement gap for those who are socially or economically disadvantaged and, potentially, any gender gaps, as active learning has been found to enhance female achievement (Brame, no date). In Chapter 10 I explore this in more depth in terms of embodied cognition. Poems and rhyming stories lend themselves to active learning and participation and this participation embeds the sounds of words and gives children the confidence to have a go at reading unknown words, because they are presented in a context.

Bramberger (2015) uses the example of 'The Cat in the Hat' (Dr Seuss); a much-loved rhyming story that encourages participation, engagement, enjoyment; allowing children to identify with the characters through accessible language, whilst including complex rhyming patterns. In this way, the process of learning to read is brought to life. The poetic devices utilised in this wonderful rhyming text, lend themselves to ensuring participation from the children as they can easily join in with repeated lines and predictable rhymes. There is plenty of opportunity for using gesture and signs, as this text is read aloud, making it very accessible, particularly for children with EAL or hearing impairments.

Performance

Performing poems is another form of active learning, which allows children to hear and enact, to observe and visualise – all key skills when learning to read. You could use a poem such as 'River' by Valerie Bloom – https://childrens.poetryarchive.org/poem/the-river/ – which has a wonderful rhythm and rhyme scheme and lends itself beautifully to performance. You could start by playing the audio version of the poem, read by the poet. You could then read it again, playing the predication game mentioned earlier – children guessing the words to end the lines. By this time, the children will have the poem embedded in their minds and you could ask them to think about how they might perform each stanza. Perhaps give each small group a stanza to work on – they could produce a freeze frame, or an action, or a movement around the classroom – and then these could be brought together for a whole class performance.

I am aware that some of these activities would not fit into the oft-allotted 20 minutes of discrete phonics teaching. However, if they were embedded across a series of sessions or carpet activities or curriculum areas – bringing subjects, objectives and topics together – it is likely that the children will benefit not just in their reading skills, but more holistically. Remember, it is our place to translate and transform the curriculum (Alexander, 2009) – not merely to deliver. All it takes is a commitment to what we know works best for our diverse learners.

The place of poetry in developing comprehension skills

When we are considering pedagogies associated with developing children's comprehension skills, we need to be sure of the purpose of reading. Ainy (2011, p. 26) defines this as the need to 'read to comprehend, realise, understand the meaning of the words that go beyond the surface, and then to be able to interpret a poem on the basis of newly achieved knowledge'. Although Ainy is explicitly referring to poetry here, I feel this is a useful definition for *all* types of reading. Key words we can take from this, which might guide our underpinning principles for teaching reading comprehension are: realise, understand and interpret.

Something we need to keep balanced in our teaching of reading is ensuring that children have a wealth of opportunities to read for pleasure (this includes being read to of course), whilst developing strong comprehension skills. Being able to understand both the obvious meaning of a text and meanings that may lie under the surface and require teasing out, are skills needed across all curriculum subjects and in all walks of life. Children need to be thoughtful, critical, reflective readers who have opinions about what they read and can share these with others. This can only happen if they receive a diet of high-quality, powerful texts, covering a range of genres; texts that excite, inform and inspire. In fact, about as far away from reading scheme, 'levelled' books as you can be. Nearly 70 years ago, Flesch (1955, cited in Bramberger, 2015) decried the methods of teaching reading – particularly the use of reading scheme books (Janet and John, Biff and Chip for example), which depicted 'totally unexciting middle-class, middle-income, middle-I.Q. children's activities'. He described these texts as harmful, leading to the exclusion of children because of the lack of relevance to their lives, thus reducing their motivation towards and interest in, reading. He invited Geisel (Dr Seuss) to write something alternative – something fun, accessible but challenging (see earlier discussion) – and thus 'The Cat in the Hat' was produced – a text that has been enjoyed by thousands for many years. And yet, scheme books prevail and we know the reasons for this – the levels are perceived to support with assessing children; parents are familiar with this type of book and may feel more able to support their children; some children enjoy the comfort of moving through the levels towards a goal – and so forth. I would argue that using poetry to develop comprehension skills is a far more effective tool and outweighs the arguments I have listed.

Poems are a world away from scheme books and are ideal texts to use to develop comprehension skills; resources which generate 'discussion, controversy and critical thinking in the classroom, rather than leading towards a stereotyped definitive interpretation of the text' (Ainy, 2011, p. 25). When children discuss poems, share their perspectives and opinions, and reflect on the views of others, they begin to use a wider range of vocabulary; indeed, different vocabulary is necessary for each poem, situation and context to allow for appropriate responses. Through this discussion, alternative interpretations emerge, so that it is not just the children waiting for the teacher to tell them what the poem means; instead, they are creating their own meanings. Reading is an interactive process where we take our own knowledge and experience to the text to help us interpret it (Ainy, 2011). Children can be encouraged to find a storyline through the poem and then think about why the poet has decided on a particular structure, to help tell this story, for example, rhyming couplets or six-line stanzas.

If you are introducing a poem on a subject the children may not know much about, you might want to support them with some research so that they come to the poem with existing knowledge. For example, if the poem was about the Caribbean, the children could use a globe or an atlas or Google Earth, explore the location, then find out about the climate, people, islands and so on. Being able to bring something to a poem is empowering and takes away the potential fear of not being able to understand the poet's intention. An initial exploration of the title is also a useful way in – why do you think it has this title? What might the poem be about? Or, you could give the children a poem with the title deleted and ask them to come up with a title (see Activity 3 later in the chapter).

Building an understanding of a poem needs to arise from an examination of how the poet has created an effect and, maybe, why. Rather than reading a poem and then asking children what they think it means (often leading to the 'guess the answer in my head' syndrome), it is more productive to read the poem and then give at least ten minutes to allow children to discuss their initial thoughts in groups and perhaps to set questions of their own. It is even better if the poem has been chosen by a child, removing the 'power' from the teacher and thereby avoiding them being seen as the font of knowledge. Pullinger and Whitley (2016, p. 322) emphasise the importance of not moving 'to the analysis stage before personal engagement has taken root' and this is where it is so important to give time for extended discussion and debate between the children, before we engage them with specific questions. When we do start to question, these need to allow for different interpretations – for example:

- Why might the poet have chosen to write a poem about this subject?
- Why do you think they used this structure and what effect does it have?
- If you could choose any topic to write a poem about, what would you choose?
- Are there particular words that make you feel something?

If our questions are too closed, we take on the role of the 'gatekeeper to meaning' (Xerri, 2015, p. 33), and children will merely try to guess the 'right answer' which they believe to be in our head, rather than feel the freedom to put forward their own ideas and opinions. Poetry is open to interpretation (to a greater or lesser extent, dependent on your viewpoint), and provides, therefore, the ideal soil in which the seeds of ideas and viewpoints can grow.

Our assessment of children's comprehension can occur through observing and engaging with the small group discussions, where the initial thoughts of the children will reveal a great deal. This can then be extended into evaluating the questions they want to ask about the poem, providing invaluable data relating to their level of comprehension. We can then use

Using poetry to develop decoding and comprehension skills

our carefully constructed questions to gain even more assessment evidence. Through all of this, we need to be aware of what exactly we are intending to assess. Comprehension – yes. But comprehension of what? This might include:

- What it is that makes a poem a poem
- Specific vocabulary
- The effect of structure
- The effect of rhyme
- How rhythm is created

Activities

Activity 1: Playful predictions

Explain to the children that you are going to read them a funny poem about a cat, but it will also be a game because you are going to stop at certain points, and their task is to guess the missing word. Ask them to raise their hand if they think they can predict the missing word.

Have a copy of Ken Nesbitt's poem, 'My Cat Goes Flying Through the Air' (www.poetry4kids.com/poems/my-cat-goes-flying-through-the-air/), displayed to the children, but with the end words of some lines erased (the words that can easily be predicted because of their relationship with the line before). As you go through the poem, record on your working wall/flipchart any words that children suggest, but at this stage, do not say whether these match the poem or not. Once you have finished the poem, play the audio version (accessed at the link above) and ask the children to listen out for any words they might have mentioned. Probably, most of their suggestions will be correct and it is good to express amazement at this point – how did you manage to do that? Hopefully, this will lead into a discussion about rhyme, context, making meaning and so on. You might also want to draw attention to words that sound the same but are spelt differently, for example, 'air' and 'there' or 'then' and 'again' (and of course this can depend on accent, which can lead to a whole different and exciting discussion!).

Explain to the children that if they get stuck on a word when they are reading, it can sometimes help to guess/predict what might come next, in the same way they have just done so successfully achieved with Nesbitt's poem. If possible, have a whole range of poems by different poets which lend themselves to this prediction exercise. You might then, depending on the age of the children, extend this into a writing session, using cloze procedure, whereby children complete the missing words. Below is an example, using Robert Louis Stevenson's poem, 'Bed in Summer'. You will see dashes where children would be expected to fill in a word.

Bed in Summer
In winter I get up at night
And dress by yellow candle - - - - -.

> In summer, quite the other way,
> I have to go to bed by - - -.
>
> I have to go to bed and see
> The birds still hopping on the - - - -,
> Or hear the grown-up people's feet
> Still going past me in the - - - - - -.
>
> And does it not seem hard to you,
> When all the sky is clear and - - - -,
> And I should like so much to play,
> To have to go to bed by - - -?
> (Robert Louis Stevenson)

You could then ask children to explore some poetry books and find rhyming poems with predictable endings to lines and they could devise a cloze procedure activity for their friends.

Activity 2: Phonics in context

This activity can be adjusted to any sounds that you are exploring with children at any moment. It can also be tweaked to make it more of a spelling investigation for older children. What you need are several poems at your disposal – start building a bank of poems by different poets, and ensure your collection is diverse – poets from different backgrounds, cultures, countries and continents (not just your favourites!). Think about including classics, more modern poems, and lesser-known examples.

For this activity, you *do* need a rhyming poem. I have used Robert Louis Stephenson's 'My Shadow':

> I have a little shadow that goes in and out with me,
> And what can be the use of him is more than I can see.
> He is very, very like me from the heels up to the head;
> And I see him jump before me, when I jump into my bed.
>
> The funniest thing about him is the way he likes to grow -
> Not at all like proper children, which is always very slow;
> For he sometimes shoots up taller like an india-rubber ball,
> And he sometimes goes so little that there's none of him at all.
>
> He hasn't got a notion of how children ought to play,
> And can only make a fool of me in every sort of way.
> He stays so close behind me, he's a coward you can see;
> I'd think shame to stick to nursie as that shadow sticks to me!

One morning, very early, before the sun was up,
I rose and found the shining dew on every buttercup;
But my lazy little shadow, like an arrant sleepy-head,
Had stayed at home behind me and was fast asleep in bed.

I would use this poem to explore the phoneme /ee/ but would take time to enjoy and explore the poem first. After an initial reading and general discussion, read the poem again, and ask the children to listen out for any sounds that occur more than once. They may well pick up on /ee/ but, if they do not, on a third reading, draw attention to this sound. Can the children think of any other words that have the same sound – note these down somewhere highly visible. The poetry4kids website – www.poetry4kids.com/ – has a rhyming dictionary which the children will really enjoy using. If you have an interactive whiteboard, volunteers could come up and type one of the words from the poem into the rhyming dictionary search box and then the site offers examples of words with the same sound. If, for example, you type in the word 'me' you get words such as 'key', 'flea', 'ski' and also some much more complex vocabulary such as 'idiosyncrasy' and 'machete', making the activity very useful for older children also.

Hopefully, children will pick up on the very different spellings for the sound /ee/ and this can lead to a powerful discussion that will open their minds to the challenges they might encounter when decoding text. They will begin to realise that the same sound can be produced by different combinations of letters. Now, return to the poem and ask children to identify the words that sound the same but where the /ee/ sound is spelt differently, for example me/see.

Activity 3: Guess the title!

Explain to the children that you are going to read them a poem, but you are not going to tell them the title. Instead, they are going to work as 'poetry investigators', looking for clues within the poem, which might indicate the title. From your growing collection, find two poems which, from the words used, indicate the main subject of the poem. You could use 'The Eagle' by Alfred, Lord Tennyson or 'Seal' by William Jay Smith. I have included 'The Eagle' below and you can access 'Seal' at: www.poemhunter.com/poem/seal-4/.

The Eagle
He clasps the crag with crooked hands;
Close to the sun in lonely lands,
Ring'd with the azure world, he stands.

The wrinkled sea beneath him crawls;
He watches from his mountain walls,
And like a thunderbolt he falls.

Read one of the poems aloud, then give each group a copy of the poem (without the title). Encourage them to look at specific language used, using dictionaries if necessary to check the meaning of words and to discuss possibilities. Plenty of time needs to be given for this, and it is an excellent opportunity to visit the groups and assess levels of comprehension, and skills of collaboration and communication. Ask the children to decide on a title and to write this on a mini whiteboard or sheet of paper, advising them that they need to nominate a group leader, who will be asked to explain and justify their choice. When all groups have written their title, give them two minutes to tour the room and take a look at the titles chosen by other groups. You do the same and write the titles on the main whiteboard.

Each group leader now explains why they decided on their title. Hopefully, this will lead to a discussion about particular words used by the poet. Often, children bring their knowledge and experience from outside school in these types of discussions, and this is to be celebrated. If the children do not mention particular key words – 'azure', 'ring'd', 'crooked hands' and 'thunderbolt' – introduce them into the discussion and draw out ideas relating to why the poet might have used these words and what effect they have.

Finally, read the poem again and then reveal the title, perhaps with an image to increase the impact. The children will of course be delighted if they guessed correctly and further discussion might be needed, so that they can reiterate how, as 'poetry investigators' they followed the clues left by the poet. If they were incorrect, it is useful to discuss what 'clues' took them down a different pathway. If time, or perhaps in another lesson, you can follow the same procedure with 'Seal' – an uplifting, joyous poem – asking a child this time to do the initial reading.

Activity 4: Poetry jumble

This is a useful activity to encourage children to be flexible about the interpretation of poetry and how the ideas might be presented on the page. Choose a poem – for older children, you could use Charles Causley's poem 'Timothy Winters' and there is an audio version read by the poet here – https://childrens.poetryarchive.org/poem/timothy-winters/. Discuss the meaning of some of the more challenging vocabulary and give the children time to chat about the whole poem in their small groups. Give each group an envelope which contains all the lines of the poem but cut up separately. They then re-assemble the poem, in any way they wish. Emphasise that they do not have to reproduce the original – theirs may well vary and this is indeed very likely. However, it needs to lead the reader through the story of Timothy Winters, so that they understand his life. Each group could then perform their poem and produce a written version so that they can all be compared. Time needs to be given for discussion of the different versions and how the changing of the order of the lines changes the experience of the reader and their understanding of Timothy's life.

If children have not had much exposure to poetry, you might want to begin with a shorter poem and perhaps do the activity altogether as a class, with you modelling some approaches. It is an activity worth doing on a regular basis, as it develops children's understanding of how poems are constructed and, through close examination of each line and where it might best 'fit', children are immersed in the poet's ideas and language and are developing their comprehension skills.

References

Ainy, S. (2011) 'A Reflection on the Use of Poetry in Developing Reading Comprehension in an EFL Classroom', *ELTED*, 14, 24–31.

Alexander, R. (2009) 'Towards a Comparative Pedagogy', in Cowen, R. & Kasamias, A. M. (ed.), *International Handbook of Comparative Education*, New York, Springer, 911–29.

Austin, R. (2021) 'Teaching Early Reading', in Bower, V. (ed.), *Debates in Primary Education*, Abingdon: Routledge, 91–106.

Bradbury, A. & Roberts-Holmes, G. (2017) *Grouping in Early Years and Key Stage 1. 'A Necessary Evil'?* (Final Report), Available at: https://neu.org.uk/sites/neu.org.uk/files/NEU279-Grouping-in-early-years-KS1.PDF. Accessed on 11.01.2022.

Bramberger, A. (2015) 'Enhancing Literacy Through Poetry: Two Historical Initiatives-revisited', *Journal of Poetry Therapy*, 28, 4, 237–249.

Brame, C. J. (no date) *Active Learning*, Available at: https://cft.vanderbilt.edu/wp-content/uploads/sites/59/Active-Learning.pdf. Accessed on 11.01.2022.

DfEE (2007) *Letters and Sounds Principles and Practice of High Quality Phonics*, London: HMSO.

Dymoke, S., Barrs, M., Lambirth, A. & Wilson, A. (eds.) (2015) *Making Poetry Happen: Transforming the Poetry Classroom*, London: Bloomsbury.

Education Endowment Foundation (no date) 'Within Class Attainment Grouping', Available at: https://educationendowmentfoundation.org.uk/education-evidence/teaching-learning-toolkit/within-class-attainment-grouping. Accessed on 12.01.2022.

Flesch, R. (1955) *Why Johnny Can't Read – And What You Can Do About It*, New York: HarperCollins.

Henry, L. (2015) 'The Effects of Ability Grouping on the Learning of Children from Low Income Homes: A Systematic Review', *The STeP Journal*, 2, 3, 70–87.

Jackson, K. (2018) 'Phonics "First and Fast"... But at What Cost?', *BERA blog*, Available at: www.bera.ac.uk/blog/phonics-first-and-fast-but-at-what-cost, Accessed on 11.01.2022.

Krashen, S. (2018) 'Does Phonics Deserve the Credit for the Improvement in PIRLS?', in Clark, M. M. (ed.), *Teaching Initial Literacy: Policies, Evidence and Ideology*, Birmingham: Glendale Education.

Ofsted (2010) *Reading by Six: How the Best Schools Do It (Report Summary)*, Available at: www.gov.uk/government/publications/reading-by-six-how-the-best-schools-do-it. Accessed on 11.01.2022.

Pullinger, D. & Whitley, D. (2016) 'Beyond Measure: The Value of the Memorised Poem', *Changing English Studies in Culture and Education*, 23, 4, 314–325.

Walker, M., Bartlett, S., Betts, H., Sainsbury, M. & Worth, J. (2014) 'Phonics Screening Check Evaluation Research Report', Available at: www.gov.uk/government/publications/phonics-screening-check-evaluation-final-report. Accessed on 13.02.2022.

Weale, S. (2022) 'Focus on Phonics to Teach Reading is 'Failing Children', Says Landmark Study', London: The Guardian.

Xerri, D. (2015) 'Case Study 1: Critical Reading and Student Engagement with Poetry', in Dymoke, S., Barrs, M., Lambirth, A. & Wilson, A. (eds.), *Making Poetry Happen: Transforming the Poetry Classroom*, London: Bloomsbury, 29–35.

4 Promoting an enjoyment of writing through poetry

Chapter 4 begins by examining why it is that poetry writing might inspire more/better writing generally, before moving on to explore two key themes relating to the teaching and learning of poetry writing – the advantages and challenges of using models and the advantages and challenges of writing freedom. The chapter concludes with four examples of activities you might use to promote an enjoyment of poetry writing and therefore – hopefully – writing more generally.

Introduction

Writing is not, of course, an activity restricted to the subject of English. Children will find times when they need to write, even in lessons which do not seem to have this as a focus. Take Physical Education for example – predominantly we want to get children moving, exercising, keeping fit. However, there are times when rules need to be recorded or scores to be kept. Tactics might need jotting down or names of team members. The ability to write confidently on a range of subjects is something we would wish for all the children we teach and, ideally, we would like them to enjoy writing. This is not, however, always the case and some children actively *dislike* writing and will find any reason not to do so. In this chapter, I will argue that a positive approach to the writing of poems (arguably, a far more manageable genre for children to explore with their writing) has the potential to ignite in children a realisation of the power of writing and what it can do for you. This then has the chance to traverse into other curriculum subjects and areas of life.

The chapter begins by examining why it is that poetry writing might inspire more/better writing generally. I then go on to explore what I consider to be two key themes relating to the teaching and learning of poetry writing – the advantages and challenges of using models and the advantages and challenges of writing freedom. The chapter concludes with four examples of activities you might use to promote an enjoyment of poetry writing and therefore – hopefully – writing more generally.

Poetry writing as a catalyst to an enjoyment of writing more generally

Why might poetry – of all the genres – provide the catalyst for this desire to write? In my experience, there are several reasons for this, and I shall discuss them here with some

DOI: 10.4324/9781003154174-5

exemplars. First, when you write a poem you can, if you choose, forget the 'normal' writing rules relating to punctuation and sentence construction. Young children must surely feel very constrained and restricted by what to them at first appear to be quite arbitrary commands to 'put a full stop here' and 'make sure you have a capital letter there', and this can be enough to sow the seeds of disenchantment with this chore called writing. To be able to say, 'Today we are going to learn about something that breaks all the rules and, guess what, you can too!' is an exciting way to start a lesson!

Michael Rosen is of course the master of breaking conventional writing rules and his poem 'Over My Toes', about standing by the sea edge, is a strong example to share with children – https://childrens.poetryarchive.org/poem/over-my-toes/ (I use this poem again in Chapter 5, for a different reason). This poem does have a capital letter at the very beginning but then every other line just starts with a lower-case letter and the focus is on the sound of the words and what they evoke – nothing to do with sentences and rules and what is right or wrong. The clever repetition and the rhythm of the lines puts you there at the seaside and there is much to be gained from just spending time listening to and feeling this poem (the link above has an audio recording of Michael reading the poem). However, it is also valuable as an example of how the 'shape' of a poem can be entirely your choice – you can make it fit the meaning or indeed, the meaning to fit the shape – whichever you prefer. Another example is William Carlos Williams's 'The Red Wheelbarrow' – www.poetryfoundation.org/poems/45502/the-red-wheelbarrow – a poem which might amuse children in its initial apparent simplicity but will hopefully provoke lively discussion – about content and form. I explore another of Williams's poems in Activity 1 later in the chapter.

By showing examples such as these, the world opens up in terms of writing possibilities, as children begin to realise that they have 'permission' to write about what interests them and can experiment with form and line length and how to put their words on the paper. This of course does not only apply to poetry writing. Confidence can spread into other genres – creative production of persuasive leaflets which might contain some poetic elements; stories which reflect the cadences and rhythms of poetry; non-fiction that recognises that, although this is a more formal, rule-bound genre, the order in which words and images are placed on the page can have a profound impact on how messages are received.

The second way that poetry writing might serve as a catalyst for other writing is that it can be perceived as more manageable and build children's confidence. This is not to say that poems are easy – to read or to write. Neither are they always short and simple to decode. However, for children there are many examples which *are* of a practicable length and not so daunting as a story for example and which, they have been told (by you of course), they can interpret in any way they wish. This might mean that a door opens which was previously closed. By starting with poems that children enjoy, that perhaps make them laugh, 'hooking' them in, we can gradually broaden their exposure and immerse them in more complicated structures and meanings. But it is the initial hook that is so important – the feeling that every one of us can enjoy poetry and write a poem and, if to begin with it is by using the style or form or subject of another poet, then that is fine – we all learn from each other. Eleanor Farjeon's poem 'Cats Sleep Anywhere' – www.scrapbook.com/poems/doc/8991.html – is an ideal example. The concept is simple and easily understood and could be used as a model for children's own ideas about pets. The in-line rhymes are quite complex and offer another layer of discussion, should you wish to explore this. Poems such as these – offering the opportunity for different approaches, dependent on your aim, the age of the children and so forth – are invaluable in your poetry collection. The section later in the chapter explores the idea of using poems as models in more depth.

So, just one more reason for now (I have plenty more!), to suggest why poetry might serve as a spark for writing more generally. And that reason is words. Vocabulary. Lexicons. When poets create poems, they take a great deal of time to think of the 'best words, in the best order' (to quote Samuel Taylor Coleridge), aiming to draw in their reader and convince them of an image or a message or a feeling. These words are the lifeblood of writing – whatever the genre. The writer who has a significant lexicon on which to draw does not have to spend time and energy constantly searching for the word to fit the setting or the character or the event. In her article focusing on the use of poetry to enhance vocabulary (in her case, within language classes), Aydınoğlu (2013, p. 274) argues that poetry is a wonderful source of language for a variety of reasons: it provides 'bountiful examples', the contexts are authentic and can appeal to all learners, language and culture are intertwined and provide an insight into our own and others' cultures, and the language is often designed to draw the reader in and appeal to emotions, feelings and senses. I agree with all these points but would also argue that mere exposure to poetry – or indeed, any other genre – is not enough. Explicit and overt identification and discussion of words is a key pedagogy to enable children to retain the new vocabulary, use it and transfer it to other contexts (even more so of course for children with English as an additional language).

So many times, visiting schools, I have seen lessons where, for the most part of an hour, the children are 'collecting' words to describe the setting of their story. Now, this is not a bad activity at all – descriptive words are much needed for this aspect of their writing. I would argue however, that a daily diet of poems, on myriad subjects, of differing lengths – sad, happy, crazy, mesmerising – will provide the vocabulary for what is essentially, a fairly basic activity for children of any age. Repeated exposure and explicit reference to new words and phrases means that, when it comes to our lesson on story settings, it takes very little time to gather some initial ideas; to spark the memories and imaginations fired up from the poems they have heard. Imagine a poem a day. Every day of the school year. That is a lot of words and a huge lexicon upon which to draw.

The suggestions discussed so far – rule-breaking, the accessibility of the genre and the power of poetry to provide extensive vocabularies – should be enough to give reluctant writers the opportunity to find different ways to express their ideas, whilst providing more able writers with the chance to extend their repertoire; to experiment and innovate. I will now move on to examine more specific approaches, based on different perspectives relating to how best to support children with their writing of poetry.

Using different approaches

In a chapter written many years ago with my colleague Sue (Bower and Barrett, 2011), we examined four different approaches to poetry writing, offered by key voices from the poetry world: Sandy Brownjohn (1994), Michael Rosen (1998), Jill Pirrie (1987) and Ted Hughes (1963). These approaches were:

- Manipulating language within a structure, focusing on words within lines, making it manageable for young poets (Brownjohn)
- Getting thoughts and feelings onto the page, with less focus on poetic techniques or form, with children's authentic voice emerging (Rosen)
- Using poetic forms and specific poems as models for children's writing – this initial constraint leading to freedom through the developing of confidence (Pirrie)
- The importance of children being exposed to a wide range of accessible poems, which appeal to the senses (Hughes)

There are of course strengths and challenges to all these approaches and, as with all pedagogies and resources, we need to judge the best way forward for the children we teach and try out different methods with the understanding that different strategies will work for some but not all. For the purpose of this chapter, I am going to focus on just two of these – Pirrie's and Rosen's – as, arguably, they fall at each end of a continuum (see Figure 4.1).

The advantages and challenges of using models to support poetry writing

Both novice and experienced writers can gain a great deal from using the writing of others as a model for their own compositions. This might mean that they adopt the structure or setting of a short story, the plot and characterisation of a novel, or (more relevant to this book) the form/style/tone/patterns of an existing poem. In this way they develop their knowledge and understanding of a particular form and gain confidence, leading ultimately to a more independent approach to writing reflecting their own unique ideas and style.

Within the whole area of using poetic form as a scaffold, there are two opposing arguments and, if I am honest, I fall between the two. This is typical of my approach to many aspects of education, as I do not find a polarisation of ideas useful and often feel that a combination of ideas, viewpoints and strategies can lead to more exciting results. What is far more important than what we as practitioners believe works, is finding out how the children want to approach a writing activity and, where possible, providing choice and letting them take the lead. It helps, however, to examine each end of the continuum in order to reach our own decisions about the approaches to take.

If we look at the far left of the continuum, the emphasis is on using models as scaffolds for children's own writing and this will be the focus of this section. It might be that you want the children to write using a specific poetic form – a kenning perhaps (see Chapter 6 for

Figure 4.1 Poems as models for writing – a continuum

discussion relating to kenning poems) – and therefore you would immerse them in examples of kennings, written on a range of topics by a variety of poets. In this way, the children absorb the cadences, style and techniques for this type of poem and can replicate it in their own writing; the poems are providing the scaffold. Or it might be that you have found a poem with a strong structure and content which you think will appeal to the children you teach, and you explore this poem in depth with the children. They then use the poem as a model for their own work (see Activity 1 later in the chapter for an example of this).

Womelsduff (2005, p. 23) describes this as 'the freedom that structure provides'. In her project, Womelsduff offered her students powerful poems as scaffolds, but then gave them choice by saying they could write about something they really loved or meant a great deal to them. The students produced high quality poems which surprised even themselves. When asked why they had felt empowered to do so, the students were very clear on what helped them – they were able to write about something that was personal to them; the poem used as a model provided a clear structure which they could imitate in their own work; they could see what their poems might look like on the page; and it did not have to rhyme. There were also guidelines for assessing each others' poems and the students found these useful for supporting their own writing. Womelsduff acknowledges that 'a rigidity of structure and formulas to approach writing tasks often results in wooden, predictable, dull student writing' (ibid., p. 23) but argues that, without strong models those new to poetry writing can struggle to get started or to have enough understanding of the genre to find their own voice within it.

Interestingly, Womelsduff uses the words, 'freedom', 'structure', 'boundaries', 'a foundation' and these are worth bearing in mind when we plan writing activities for children and consider what level of support will be most useful and what degree of autonomy the children are ready for. Sometimes the support provided by a strong, recognisable 'frame' – a rhyming couplet for example – provides a neat, self-contained unit which may make poetry writing feel more manageable. Irresistible rhythms and catchy rhyme schemes, repetition and refrains – all these can be comforting for young writers and give them the confidence to have a go.

As with all scaffolding (Bruner, 1966), there comes a time when it needs to be removed, to allow children more freedom and agency with their writing; in this way, poetic forms are the 'stepping stones' to independence (Wilson, 2007, p. 448). Some children may be ready for this scaffolding to be removed very quickly and, indeed, may never have relied on it! I remember when I used 'this is just to say' by William Carlos Williams (see Activity 1 later in the chapter) with a Year 6 class (ten- and eleven-year-olds). The idea was to utilise this poem as a model for their own writing, in any way they wished. About half the class followed the structure, stanza length and so on to the letter; about a quarter took some elements of Williams' poem but inserted their own modifications; and the others did not use anything stylistically from the original and proceeded to write in their own style and form (and some of these were strikingly unique) whilst using the same theme (asking for forgiveness). This was an enlightening moment for me as I realised that for some, writing confidence is almost inherent or merely needs a prompt; for others the use of a scaffold and subsequent removal of this support needs to be more sensitive and gradual. Even more telling was the way we can never predict the direction children will go in!

When using poems as models, the balance between content and form needs to be something overtly discussed with children. If the balance falls too much towards form, children focus entirely on achieving this rather than what they want the poem to be about. This can often happen with the writing of haiku poems, where children are so caught up with achieving the traditional 5-7-5 syllable count for the three lines, that they lose sight of the message they are conveying in the poem. Or, when they are working so much on making a poem rhyme that they lose focus on the meaning of the word they are using (this often happens when children are largely exposed to rhyming poems). Wilson and Dymoke (2017, p. 131) remind us that 'the form, vocabulary and tone of a poem are all saturated with its meaning' and this is a message we need to remember ourselves and communicate to our young writers.

Engaging in modelled writing, where the person doing the modelling (this could be you, a classroom assistant, a child or a visiting poet) talks through the writing decisions they are making in real time, is a powerful strategy (Bower and Barrett, 2011). If we return to the haiku example, you might be modelling word choice:

> I really want to use the word magnificent in my second line, but this would take the line to eight syllables rather than seven. I think in this case, to create the effect I am wanting, I'll use it anyway as it works so well. We do not always need to follow the traditional rules – because it is our poem!

Explicitly discussing this decision-making process gives children 'permission' to make their own choices and immersing them in a large range of poems, which reflect the poetic form they are experimenting with, will help them to realise that an individual approach is very acceptable. Within these discussions, encouraging children to question how a poet achieves a particular effect and what impact a word or a line or a stanza has on us as the reader, will support them with a reflective, evaluative approach to their own writing and a more positive view of editing and re-writing. This also allows them to escape what Wilson describes as the potential for literary models to be 'more straitjacket than scaffold' (Wilson, 2007, p. 453), where the writer feels constrained by the form presented.

The advantages and challenges of writing freedom

We are of course never entirely free – whether it is in terms of our thoughts, our actions, our writing. All of these are influenced by our lives, experiences, relationships, schooling, culture, language, economic status and so forth. What I mean by this is, if we say to children, 'write a poem about anything you like, using any form you wish' their choices will of course be influenced by any number of factors. They may also find this extremely daunting, either because the choices are infinite or because no ideas immediately spring to mind. They may eagerly grab paper or iPad or laptop, settle themselves down in a quiet corner and start 'penning' their ideas. This, I suspect, is what we tend to find quite daunting as practitioners as, on the one hand we might be anxious to give autonomy and allow children space to create, whilst on the other we are aware that this can cause anxiety and 'blank page syndrome', not to mention the pressure of achieving particular objectives within the curriculum.

Grainger, Goouch and Lambirth (2003) conducted a project entitled 'We're Writers' which sought to hear children's voices in terms of their writing, in an environment where teachers' approaches to writing were influenced by the standards agenda and teaching for tests. The teachers were concerned that children were merely jumping through the hoops when writing, rather than immersing themselves in it and enjoying the process. Key themes emerging from the research indicated that attitudes towards and perceptions of writing varied across age groups (younger children responded more positively, Year 3 and Year 4 children more negatively and Year 5 and Year 6 children with some ambivalence and at times, indifference); and children were very keen to be given more choice regarding their writing topics. Some older writers 'seemed to see themselves as passive recipients, disengaged from the process of becoming writers and with little sense of their own agency or empowerment' (ibid., p. 8), and this was of great concern to the teachers involved in the project. Grainger, Goouch and Lambirth conclude by suggesting the idea of a 'negotiated curriculum' (ibid., p. 12), to ensure that children's voices are heard and responded to, and this is where decisions must be carefully made with regards to the poems we choose and the balance between scaffolding and freedom.

There are straightforward and fun ways around this, whereby autonomy can be granted but only once the vital groundwork is completed. This foundational practice includes regular and frequent reading of poems to children – first thing in the morning, during assemblies, whilst waiting for the call to lunch, when a lesson finishes ahead of time, during a five-minute slot each day allocated to poetry, at the end of the day instead of a 3 o'clock story – many opportunities. The benefit of poems is that they often take mere seconds to read and yet the impact is considerable. Regular reading of poems ensures that children become immersed in rhythms, cadences, rhymes, feelings, sounds, experiences. They begin to recognise particular forms, to express their enjoyment of particular poets, to offer to read poems they have discovered or indeed, their own poems. They remember poems about different subjects and they 'borrow' the vocabulary. They have rhymes ingrained in their memories which they can weave into their own poems. If poetry reading is part of the timetable, when it comes to poetry writing, children have a vast repertoire to draw on in terms of their own ideas and they are building the scaffolds towards future writing freedom.

It is worth remembering that, with any writing we are asking children to undertake, freedom can come in different forms. Where possible, allow children the following choices:

- The implement they choose to write/type with
- The size/colour/type of paper/screen
- The place to write
- The time to write
- With whom they choose to write
- Silence or background music

Here is a brief example: I created a set of poetry writing paper. These were A4 sheets of various colours, and they had different borders (easy to produce on a Word document) which I felt would appeal to the children in my class – footballers, animals, sweets, shapes, different colours and so forth. These went into special 'writing trays' and the children could help themselves to their choice of paper. In another tray were a wide range of writing implements – felt tip pens, crayons, glitter pens (a real hit!), coloured pencils and so on. Again, children could

Promoting an enjoyment of writing through poetry

choose to write using any of these or a selection (when possible, I also gave them the choice to produce poems on iPads, laptops or PCs). This incurred a great deal of excitement and discussion and the children could not wait to write – a scenario you definitely want to promote! They went on to produce wonderful work which they framed and displayed. They also often arrived in class with paper they had decorated with borders of their choice, or they produced these for their friends who selected their own style.

Freedom, therefore, can come in different guises and it is about looking out for these opportunities and responding to the individual needs of the children you teach. Below are some activities which I hope will provide practical suggestions for how these ideas about freedom and the earlier ideas about using models and poetic form, might manifest themselves in your poetry writing pedagogies.

Activities

Activity 1: This is just to say

The following activity is based around the poem 'this is just to say' by William Carlos Williams – https://poets.org/poem/just-say – and fits into the approach discussed earlier in the chapter, where poems are used as models for children's own writing. I have used this particular poem successfully with children aged from six to 11 and with adults of all ages – it has great appeal! It is the most wonderful poem for so many reasons. First, it is a message, or maybe a note, from the poet to somebody – maybe his wife or friend – admitting to an everyday act, with which we are all familiar – eating something that was meant to be shared! (You could, if you wanted to engage children in a deeper analysis, focus on universal themes such as guilt and temptation, but this is not the aim of this activity.) If we want to get children enjoying writing, then appealing to a recognisable human weakness is a good way to start. Second, it is a short, readable poem; very accessible to all. Third, it has an absence of traditional punctuation (typical of the poet's style) and therefore breaks the familiar 'rules' of the classroom – another joy for children!

Read the poem and then allow the children time to discuss in pairs or groups. Come back together as a class and use these questions (or your own) as prompts:

- What do you notice about the poem (absence of punctuation, capital letters, unusual layout etc.)?
- Why do you think the poet writes in this way?
- Do you like this style?
- What is the poem about?

Ask the children to discuss in groups any times in their lives where they have had to be forgiven for something they have done. Elect a leader for each group and they choose their favourite anecdote to share with the class.

Play the 30-second video of Matthew Macfadyen acting out the poem in a real-life scenario – www.youtube.com/watch?v=Od5bLfOgq2Q. What do the children think about this? A poem as a note?

Show the class an example of a poem that you have written in the same style, or use this one that I wrote for my class:

>
> this is just to say
> i have not completed
> my homework
> which was due in
> today
>
> and which
> you are probably
> waiting
> to mark
>
> forgive me
> the sun was so warm
> and my new bike
> so tempting
> (Virginia Bower)

Discuss the format and how the original poem can be used as a template (if they wish to do so). It is important to emphasise that this format does not have to be strictly adhered to – it can be used merely as a guide – otherwise the children can become frustrated with not being able to find the 'correct' word or line length.

Children can then work in pairs or individually to produce their own poems in the style of Williams. They can choose how they might present these poems – as a cartoon strip perhaps, or an audio recording or short film in the style of Macfadyen's version (see Chapter 8 for more ideas on multimodal representation of poems).

Activity 2: Using haiku

Haiku poems are a real joy to share with children and to gain their responses. The idea of a haiku is to represent the absolute essence of something – generally related to nature. Within just a few words, a picture is presented of an aspect of the natural world, evoking sights, sounds and scents in a matter of seconds, potentially transporting the reader to other places or times. This for me is what poetry is all about – opening up the world and its possibilities. Ideally, the following activity would be conducted over three or four days, to give plenty of time for discussion, production and presentation.

Explain to the children the traditional features of haiku poetry – three lines; the numbers of syllables in each line; the fact that they are focused on one subject – often an object, creature or an aspect of the natural world. However, discuss the fact that poetry is very personal and, when they write their haiku poems, they can vary the syllable count or line length if it better suits their ideas. I do think this is an important point to make because otherwise children can tend to focus entirely on the number of syllables and insert words for this reason only, rather than considering the more important element which is presenting the very essence of an idea through their poem.

Use Matsuo Bashô's poem: *Frog Haiku*, which I present below in Japanese and English:

古池や 蛙飛び込む 水の音
Furuike ya
Kawazu tobikomu
Mizu no oto

The old pond
A frog leaps in.
Sound of the water.

Give children time to discuss the poem and, if you are intending to have several lessons leading up to the writing of their own, they could perhaps spend some time putting together a display with Bashô's poem as a central aspect and producing illustrations of *Frog Haiku*.

Where do you think the idea for this poem originated? Gather children's ideas. Explain that, with haiku poems, you need a strong starting point, where the visual image is clear in your mind. In this way you will have more chance of choosing the best words to represent this image. Show the class some photographs that have a particular meaning for you – it might be a holiday landscape, a flower in your garden, a family member or pet. Describe the photograph and provide the 'back story', for example 'I was on holiday in Scotland and I climbed to the top of a mountain. The views were unbelievable, with the sunlight bouncing off the loch and people and cars like toys below'. Write this description on the board and then undertake modelled writing to demonstrate how a photograph as a stimulus and an oral or written description can be turned into a haiku poem:

A tough mountain trek
Stunning views to loch and moor
Human specks below.

Children can then bring in their own photos or use online images to go through the same process. If they would rather, they can use their memory of a meaningful event in their lives, or something funny/sad/exciting they have experienced and base their haikus on this. Once haiku poems have been written, they can be added to the prepared display board.

Activity 3: Writing alternative versions

This activity is another that uses existing poems as models. Because of this, it is quite prescriptive, and I have discussed the strengths and challenges of this earlier in the chapter. Always consider what stage children are at with their writing confidence and let this influence the activities you choose. This example can give children a great deal of confidence and is a useful shared writing activity.

It is always good to have activities for particular times of year and this is designed for the Christmas term. Read the children "Twas the Night Before Christmas' and/or play the animated film you can find here - www.youtube.com/watch?v=NF6gMctT3XI.

Explain to the class that they are going to create an alternative version of this poem entitled "Twas the Day After Christmas'. Model a possible beginning:

> 'Twas the day after Christmas,
> And all through the town
> Children were playing,
> As snow fluttered down;
> Brand new sledges
> All on display,
> Shrieks of excitement,
> On this Boxing Day.
> (Virginia Bower)

What has been retained from the original? Discuss rhythm and rhyme and the 'feel good' element of the poem.

Ask children to work in groups to come up with ideas for the next stanza or, with younger children, work as a class. Gather vocabulary on the whiteboard and ideas that the children want included. Work together to produce the next part of the poem. If children seem confident, they could go on to create their own stanzas.

Activity 4: Collaborative writing

Earlier in the chapter I discussed the idea of poetry writing as a social activity and how, as poets, we 'borrow' words and ideas from others. Encouraging collaborative writing can take away any negative feelings towards writing poems or indeed, writing more generally. This next activity is not only collaborative but also provides quite a degree of freedom - an aspect discussed earlier in the chapter. How much freedom is up to you in terms of title choices/timings/materials used - you know your class!

Prepare the classroom by having different colour sheets of paper on each table and a range of writing implements. Tell the children that everyone is going to help each other to write poems and the subject matter can be their choice or they can choose from a list provided. The list might include:

- Autumn
- The Day I Met a Dinosaur
- My Sister
- When I'm Grown Up
- Trees
- First Day at School

Explain that they will go to a piece of paper of their choice and write a title and the first one or two lines of a poem on that paper. Model an example:

> **First Day at School**
> I stand in the playground
> All alone
>
> Once they are happy with what they have written, they leave the paper on the desk and move around the room, looking at the writing of their peers. When they find a title and first line/s that appeal to them, they add another one or two lines to the existing writing. For example, if they like the title and two lines modelled above, they could continue on this theme:
>
> **First Day at School**
> I stand in the playground
> All alone
> My heart is pounding
> My legs are weak.
>
> Emphasise the fact that the poems can be in any style. They do not need to rhyme. They can take the poem in any direction they wish.
>
> This movement from one poem to another continues until they have added to several poems. You will be undertaking the activity with the children, making sure that all poems have some contributions. When you feel the children are perhaps running out of steam, ask them to have a final look and see if they can finish one of the poems. Children then return to their original, have a read through and, if they wish, add to it or finish the poem.
>
> Discuss the ideas that have been contributed. Do the children like how their poem has evolved? Did it go in the way they envisaged? Would anybody like to read their poem? What has been useful about collaborating?

References

Aydınoğlu, N. (2013) 'Integration of Poetry with Vocabulary Teaching', *Mediterranean Journal of Educational Research*, 14a, 274-284.
Bower, V. & Barrett, S. (2011) 'Using Poetic Form: An Approach to Poetry Writing in the Primary Classroom', in Bower, V. (ed.), *Creative Ways to Teach Literacy Ideas for Children Aged 3 to 11*, London: Sage, 45-54.
Brownjohn, S. (1994) *To Rhyme or Not to Rhyme?* London: Hodder & Stoughton.
Bruner, J. (1966) *Toward a Theory of Instruction*, Cambridge, MA: Harvard University Press.
Grainger, T., Goouch, K. & Lambirth, A. (2003) 'Playing the Game Called Writing: Children's Views and Voices', *English in Education*, 37, 2, 4-14.
Hughes, T. (1963) *Here Today*, London: Hutchinson.
Pirrie, J. (1994) *On Common Ground: A Programme for Teaching Poetry*, Godalming: World Wildlife Fund.
Rosen, M. (1998) *Did I Hear You Write?*, Nottingham: Five Leaves Publications.
Wilson, A. (2007) 'Finding a Voice? Do Literary Forms Work Creatively in Teaching Poetry Writing?', *Cambridge Journal of Education*, 37, 441-457.
Wilson, A. & Dymoke, S. (2017) 'Towards a Model of Poetry Writing Development as a Socially Contextualised Process', *Journal of Writing Research*, 9, 2, 127-150.
Womelsduff, D. (2005) 'The Paradox of Structure and Freedom: An Experiment in Writing Poet', *English Journal*, 94, 4, 23-27.

5 The power of poetry to promote a multicultural, multilingual approach

This chapter begins with a focus on making connections between poetry and languages, highlighting how poetry can be the ideal resource for drawing attention to language – whether this be the linguistic diversity of our pupils or the foreign language we have decided on for curriculum coverage. Within this section there are specific suggestions for the use of collocation, lexical sets and cognates. The chapter then moves on to exploring how we might use poems in different languages, to promote and celebrate linguistic diversity, before doing the same for a celebration of different cultures. The chapter ends with three activities to set you off on your journey towards a poetry-inspired, multilingual, multicultural classroom!

Introduction

My doctoral thesis and two of my publications – *Supporting Pupils with EAL in the Primary School* (Bower, 2017) and *Language Learning and Intercultural Understanding in the Primary School* (Cobb and Bower, 2022) – focus upon language and culture and children living and learning in multilingual, multicultural contexts. It is an area that has been of interest and importance to me for many years and, whenever I discuss education or write about it, I always try to draw attention to linguistic and cultural diversity, to promote the idea that, as teachers, we can use our privileged position to overtly celebrate this diversity, within and across the curriculum. This holds true with poetry; in fact, it could be argued that this is the perfect conduit through which to explore our diverse world, as poets tend to write from perspectives that are unique and personal, whilst including messages that are universal and applicable to all.

One of my arguments is that taking a multilingual approach to our teaching and learning has the potential to expand and extend the world to our pupils; to build a community of learners who are excited by diversity and who can empathise with others in a way that enables them to celebrate difference whilst supporting those who might be settling into new lives, new cultures, new languages. By a multilingual approach, I do not mean that everything we do in school needs to be presented in more than one language. Rather, it is about seizing every opportunity to raise the status of language – particularly languages other than English – and to go far beyond 'tolerating' or 'accepting' different cultures by overtly championing and celebrating them. In this chapter, I hope to offer ideas on how we might do this using poetry.

The chapter begins with a focus on connecting poetry and languages, highlighting how poetry can be the perfect resource for drawing attention to language – whether this be the linguistic diversity of our pupils or the foreign language we have decided on for curriculum coverage. Within this section there are specific suggestions for the use of collocation, lexical sets and cognates. I then move on to exploring the particular use of poems in different languages, to promote and celebrate linguistic diversity, before doing the same for a celebration of different cultures. The chapter ends with three activities to set you off on your journey towards a poetry-inspired, multilingual, multicultural classroom!

Poetry and languages

It could be argued that everything we do in the classroom is based on language – oral and written. I would like to make a small change to this and say 'everything we do in the classroom is based on *languages*' to ensure a multilingual approach as outlined in the introduction to this chapter. Either way, using poetry to highlight and illuminate the language of the curriculum (in our case, English) and the languages of our children and school community, is one of the strongest weapons in our armoury. To illustrate this, here are three quotes from much-revered poets:

> 'Poetry: the best words in the best order' (Samuel Taylor Coleridge)
> 'Poetry is the rhythmical creation of beauty in words' (Edgar Allen Poe)
> 'Poetry is language at its most distilled and most powerful' (Rita Dove)

There is very little that cannot be taught through poetry (and this, of course, is the idea underpinning this whole book!) and this is because, to be successful and fulfilled learners, we need a strong command over language; and poetry provides this. Having words at our disposal – to engage with others, convey meaning, establish and articulate our conceptual understanding, make jokes, show our appreciation, describe our feelings, support others, express our opinions – opens doors to other people, places and opportunities. To empower children in this way is something that lies within our scope as teachers and poetry can support us in our endeavours.

Regular exposure to poetry equals regular exposure to a wealth of vocabulary – invaluable for our native English speakers and our English as an additional language (EAL) learners. Cummins (1979, 1981) introduced the idea of the different types of language required by young EAL learners – Basic Interpersonal Communication Skills (BICS) and Cognitive Academic Language Proficiency (CALP), in order to successfully navigate and participate in all aspects of school life. Although Cummins' work focuses on EAL learners, I would argue that the acquisition of these two aspects of language is essential for *all* children, when we note that between 5 and 10 per cent of children in the United Kingdom have communication disorders (The Good Schools Guide, 2021).

When we are considering using poetry to enhance language acquisition and development and to promote a more multilingual approach in our classrooms for all children, it is important to choose resources carefully. Recognising that different poems are useful for different purposes and of course, that poems do not need to have a use – more importantly, they can simply be enjoyed! – is an important aspect when selecting resources. One example of this is the choice of text you decide to read at the end of the school day. It is inadvisable to select a story or poem which has deep or complex themes, whereby the children may go home with questions or concerns that they have not had time to express and articulate. In a similar way, some poems are more valuable for those children further on with their language journey, whilst others are better utilised with those at the earlier stages. Below are two examples: the first is an activity very suitable for encouraging native speakers of English to think about language and how it can be used, and the second uses a poem that would be more useful for those learning a new language.

One of our most loved English poets – Michael Rosen – uses language in delightful and playful ways. In his poem, 'Alligator Problem' – https://childrens.poetryarchive.org/poem/alligator-problem/ – Rosen uses words such as 'rotivator', 'excavator' and 'motivator' – all four syllable words that wrap around the tongue in a very appealing way. Rosen, in typical style, is having a game with words here and asks the reader to solve this word problem and consider what an alligator does if an 'excavator excavates' and so forth. There is so much to be explored here in terms of language (as well as having a great deal of fun reciting and perhaps learning lines by heart for a performance). Children could find meanings for unfamiliar words, discuss why indeed an alligator does not 'alligate' (or perhaps they do!), and we can start to imagine what this 'alligating' might look like! Now, this poem is ideal for native speakers of English, to push them with expanding their vocabulary and having fun with the ideas. It may not be so effective however for our EAL learners, who may find that access to more commonly used vocabulary – although again through poetry – is more useful to support their progress with the English language. So, here is another example of a Michael Rosen poem which provides more 'regular' words as part of a lexicon associated with the seaside.

The poem is 'Over My Toes' (you might remember this from Chapter 4), which you can access here – https://childrens.poetryarchive.org/poem/over-my-toes/. This poem features vocabulary more likely to be known to children: 'sand', 'toes', 'sea', 'slip', 'slide' and 'slap'. It has the potential to be represented pictorially (see Chapter 8 for a discussion of the use of poetry and multimodality), to be acted out (making the concepts more accessible for EAL learners) and with very little difficulty it might be translated into a range of languages. There is repetition, alliteration and use of homophones (sea/see), and the overall impact of the poem, appealing to the senses, is considerable. The poem can be made accessible for all with very little effort and is suitable for all ages – what a gem of a resource!

Moving forward with a curriculum that has languages at its core involves a consideration of strategies that support children either with their learning and/or development of English or another language. I am going to introduce three strategies now – collocation, lexical sets and cognates – and link them with poetry to show how this genre can be a powerful tool for language development.

Collocation

When learning any language – and in your classroom this might be for EAL learners or for all learners in foreign language lessons – recognising and using collocation is a valuable strategy and draws attention to useful vocabulary. Collocation is where particular words

Using poetry to promote a multicultural, multilingual approach 61

tend to occur with other words (Xiao and McEnery, 2006), and can be *verb* collocations, for example 'Please be sure to come prepared for a swimming lesson tomorrow' (to come prepared) or *adjective-abstract noun* collocations, for example 'utter joy', 'absolute agony' or *adjective-common noun* collocations, for example 'heavy traffic', 'deep blue sea'. Try your hand at thinking of more – you will be surprised how many we use in oral and written language, without realising it!

Native speakers of a language will have an understanding, built up from birth, of *appropriate* collocation; for example, we might say 'deep sea' but we are unlikely to say 'deep sky'. When learning a new language, we will not have this implicit understanding of collocation and need therefore to meet words in appropriate contexts on a number of occasions alongside words with which they collocate – poems are a great asset here. It is rare that, by learning a single word, the semantics will be understood. Words gain their meaning from the other words around them, their position in the sentence (line, in the case of poems), and their existence within a particular context. There are higher probabilities of *certain* words occurring together, and language learners are required to develop an awareness of the possibilities that might be available and the most likely option in a particular context.

There is a lovely poem called 'Billy McBone' by Allan Ahlberg – https://childrens.poetry archive.org/poem/billy-mcbone/ – which contains useful examples of collocations – 'mind of his own', 'between his ears' and 'under lock and key'. The meaning of these phrases can be explored and discussed and, once you have started to draw your own and children's attention to them, you are all likely to start noticing examples in different texts accessed. This raising awareness about language is something that can be incorporated in all subject areas and, if you have children with EAL in your class, they can teach examples from their own language and language investigations can be set up to see which collocations do translate across into other languages and those that are simply untranslatable!

Lexical sets

Groups of words that are connected by a common theme are known as lexical sets; for example, a lexical set associated with the theme 'On the farm' might be 'tractor', 'farmer', 'field', 'animals', 'crops', 'barn', 'cow', 'sheep', 'combine harvester' and so on. If children can begin to 'collect' lexical sets, and 'study vocabulary systematically and in meaningful contexts' (Hashemi and Gowdasiaei, 2005, p. 357) this will support their oral and written language development and their understanding of how and when particular words should be used. If they can do this in more than one language, even better! Keeping with the farm theme, there is a poem for younger children at – www.littlegiraffes.com/farm.html – entitled 'Farm Alphabet' and it has a line for each letter of the alphabet and each line is connected with farms, for example 'B is for the barn where animals live'. A useful activity would be to create a lexical set of all the key words in the poem – 'barn', 'farmer', 'lambs', 'eggs', 'rooster' and so forth – and then, with the children, translate them into a target language (one under study in your foreign language lessons or a language spoken by children in your class). You could then re-write the poem, perhaps as a shared writing exercise, replacing key words in English with the translated words in another language. A multilingual poem! This has untold benefits including embedding a lexical set into discussions, exploring words in different languages, enjoying the regular pattern of a poem and having a poem as a model for children's own writing (see Chapter 4 for more discussion on this). Subjects which need very specific vocabulary – science for example – will really benefit from a regular focus on lexical sets. In Chapter 6, I give an example of using lexical sets in science, based on animals and their habitats, to create list poems.

Cognates

Another excellent practice is to draw children's attention to cognates. These are where words are similar in different languages, in terms of how they sound/are written and their meaning; for example in Spanish the word 'centre' is 'centro' and in French the word 'music' is 'musique'. Powerful pedagogy includes discussion of cognates with ALL children across ALL subject areas, drawing on pupils' knowledge where possible, for example 'I wonder what the word is for animal is in Spanish?' If you have a Spanish speaker in your class, I am sure they will be delighted to tell the class that it is 'animal'! In this way, children begin to see their language as one of many, all important, all different, yet, in some ways similar. Carlos et al. (2004) found that a combination of teaching specific vocabulary, contextualising it within reading and then allowing children to encounter the vocabulary independently promoted a higher level of comprehension. Identifying cognates and making links across languages can promote use of a more extensive vocabulary (in more than one language) and children are also more likely to make a connection when they meet words incidentally in different contexts.

Bringing poetry into these discussions might involve asking children to do a cognates investigation around a particular subject – animals for example. Each group could study a particular language and find out if cognates occur. For example, in German there are some useful examples:

Hen	Huhn
Cat	Katze
Pig	Schwein (see if children make the link with swine – older children might know this word)
Tiger	Tiger
Elephant	Elefant
Kangaroo	Känguru

Once they have collected their word lists, they could do a search online for poems about animals in their chosen language – there are some useful Spanish poems here – www.spanishplayground.net/spanish-poems-for-kids/ – French poems here – www.learn-french-help.com/french-poems-for-children.html – and poems in German here – www.mamalisa.com/?t=el&lang=German. They could do a cognate search within these poems and perhaps try to match some of the cognates they had in their lists with those in the poems. Any word and language investigations such as these are powerful pedagogies to implement and, combined with poetry, enhance the language experience for children. The next section looks in a little more detail at how you might use poems in different languages.

Poems in different languages

Throughout the book, I advocate reading at least one poem a day to your class. I cannot see a time when this would not be possible (even if or indeed, *because* Ofsted are knocking on the door!). Poems can be chosen that take just seconds to read and yet leave a lasting thought or memory in children's minds. In this section, I argue that some of these sharing opportunities could utilise poems in different languages. This may seem alien to you and your first thought might be, 'How can I read a poem in a language I am not familiar with?' You might be concerned that, if the poem uses an unfamiliar alphabet (Cyrillic or Arabic perhaps) or a non-alphabetic orthography (Chinese or Tamil) you could not read them at all.

There are several ways to approach this. Recordings of poems being read are available in many places online and this allows you to sit back and enjoy listening to a poem being read in another language. If you visit 'Mama Lisa's World' – www.mamalisa.com/?t=hubeh – you can search for songs and rhymes by country or by continent or by language. Activity 1, later in the chapter, provides an example of how you might use this resource to explore poems in different languages. Another approach to this is identifying children in your class who know poems and songs and rhymes in their first language and are happy to share and teach their peers. Older children, who are literate in their home language, may be confident to translate a poem from English and then read this to the class. This would be incredibly powerful, as all the children would then have access to the same ideas presented in the poem, but in two languages.

Parents and other members of the local community who speak different languages can be invited in to read and share poems with your class. Finding out who these people might be is sometimes the most difficult part, as often these linguistic skills go unnoticed and unexploited, and members of the community are unlikely to just present these language gifts unless approached. In my experience however, when people are asked if they might be prepared to read to children in a language other than English, they are usually very happy to do so. A brief newsletter (translated into the languages of your school community) seeking support with this is often the way forward and then word soon spreads. Members of the community might have poems that they enjoy or are familiar to them from their childhoods, which they can share. Alternatively, *you* can source poems for others to read.

But you may still be questioning what is to be gained from listening to or reading poems in different languages. My first argument is that it highlights to children the centrality of language in people's lives and that, whether you are born in Australia or Spain, Russia or Portugal, Slovenia or Chile, you will have access to poems in your own and others' languages. Poetry can be a uniting bond; a porthole revealing a different place; a way into people's minds and hearts. Discovering a familiar poem in a different language is intriguing, and discussions might be promoted relating to how ideas translate and whether the meaning changes; and how does the rhyme scheme work if the words are different?

Another reason for exploring poems and rhymes, chants and songs in different languages is that it can improve our access to these languages and be a first step into a multilingual world. As soon as I mention this, you might be thinking of classics such as 'Frère Jacques' or '*Tête, épaules, genoux et pieds*' (Head, shoulders, knees and toes), and with the wonderful world of global communications, there are plenty more out there which we can access in many more languages. This website, for example, has some favourite nursery rhymes in Spanish – https://spanishmama.com/favorite-nursery-rhymes-in-spanish/. For older children, there is a wonderful poem by Pablo Neruda, called *'Oda a los Calcetines'*/'Ode to My Socks' and you can access this in both languages here – http://poetshouse.blogspot.com/2006/06/oda-los-calcetines-ode-to-socks.html.

There is also a video of the poem being read beautifully in English here – www.youtube.com/watch?v=1GOkypeafdM. Unfortunately, I could not find a Spanish version of the poem being read but there is a powerful version in Spanish of another of Neruda's poems – 'Keeping Quiet' – here – www.youtube.com/watch?v=NGdz8haFO2I – and there is so much to explore with both poems – in terms of ideas, language use and universal concerns for humanity, relevant to all.

I have provided a few ideas here around how to use poems in different languages but be innovative yourself and consider approaches that you have not tried before, by drawing on your children and the local community. This will bring a new and powerful dimension to your pedagogy and practice and take you another step forward towards achieving a multilingual classroom, where linguistic diversity is celebrated.

Poetry and different cultures

Alongside championing linguistic diversity, we need to celebrate cultural diversity and have always a consideration of our children's lives as we choose our resources, create our plans and decide how we intend to transform the curriculum to suit our young learners. For us all, this is about recognising that we are part of the human race and will therefore have much in common; but with an awareness that we are also all very different. This difference is influenced by where we live and have lived, our family life, education, language experience, religion, beliefs, values, experiences, what we have read, watched, listened to and so forth. Poetry contains all of this and again, I have chosen three quotes to encapsulate this:

> 'Poetry is a matter of life, not just a matter of language' (Lucille Clifton)
> 'Poetry lifts the veil from the hidden beauty of the world, and makes familiar objects be as if they were not familiar' (Percy Bysshe Shelley)
> 'A poem begins in delight and ends in wisdom' (Robert Frost)

Often, when we think about the term cultural diversity, we think of children and their families whose home culture is very different to that with which we are familiar, because their heritage differs to our own. For example, we might say, 'Well, that is a very typical approach to disciplining children in Nepal', or 'Yes, often our Polish children tend to have a very strong work ethic because of their background'. These are of course huge generalisations and I only put these examples forward here because I want to argue that although some differences *are* more obvious – particularly if children and their families originate from places about which we know very little – *any* and *every* child in our class comes from a different home culture – even if they are born in the same town as us or even live in the same road. This of course is the absolute joy of getting to know our pupils really well and encouraging every opportunity for them to share aspects of their home culture (if they are happy to do so). The

Using poetry to promote a multicultural, multilingual approach 65

fact that some of these 'sharings' *will* be very different to our own experiences is of course a bonus and exploring poetry from different backgrounds is part of this. Because of the exciting nature of cultures very different to our own, I want to discuss some ways you might explore this.

There is a wonderful site which explores ten poets from different countries and cultures – Poland, Turkey, South Africa, France, Italy, Spain, Lebanon, Switzerland, United States and Nepal – www.sbs.com.au/language/english/ten-poets-from-different-cultures-worth-reading. Some of the poems presented could certainly be used with children in your classes, but I share this website more for the information about the poets themselves. Raising our own interest in poets and poems will enable us better to support the children we teach, and it is human nature to enjoy reading a little about people's lives and what motivates them. This site provides just this – with a snippet of biography, an image/photo and one of their poems. You could show children a section of this site which you think is appropriate for their age, and suggest that, as a class they produce a similar web page with their favourite poets. Activity 2, towards the end of this chapter, goes into more detail about how you might do this, but for now I want to provide two examples of ways to focus on poetry from different cultures.

Hearing the voices of those from a range of backgrounds adds a richness to the experience for the children – they not only enjoy the poems presented to them, but they are better placed to hear the voice of the poet and to understand where the ideas originate. An excellent way to explore this is to use the Children's Poetry Archive. This site provides some details about the poets and then examples of their poems, with recordings of the poets reading them. One you might want to explore is the poet John Agard and you can find details about his life and readings of five of his poems here – https://childrens.poetryarchive.org/poet/john-agard/. One of these poems is '*Quipu Chant*' and, before he reads the poem, Agard provides some background to the ideas presented. The poem introduces the reader to a different culture and fascinating cultural practices. This could lead to extended discussions around family and cultural traditions, ways of recording, celebrating and so on and would provide the perfect starting point for an investigation. But most importantly, it provides a new lens through which to see the world, beyond our own imaginings or experience.

The second poet you might want to explore with children is Valerie Bloom. There is an interview with this poet on the Children's Poetry Archive website and Bloom talks about the influences on her writing and how she goes about writing poems. The children can listen to the interview and there is also a transcript to allow them to follow along or return to in their own time. On Bloom's page – https://childrens.poetryarchive.org/interviews/an-interview-with-valerie-bloom/ – there are recordings of three of her poems – 'Granny Is' (which I discuss in Chapter 1), 'Frost' (wonderful use of imagery) and 'The River' (this has a powerful rhythm and use of repetition, which children might want to use in their own poems). Imagine if you were able to explore a poet a week, through the school year, during timetabled lessons, early morning work, homework, holiday projects – whenever you could fit it in. What an exposure to different cultures this would lead to. Children would have a better understanding of how all our lives are unique, whilst having the opportunity to recognise how aspects of life are universal and familiar. As you become more aware of poets' work and their style and subject matter, it might be that you can take a more planned approach to the poets you introduce at particular times of year, to enable connections to be made across curriculum areas and topics.

Here are some other resources that might prove useful:

- The BBC have an interesting page – 'Roots and Water 1: Poetry from other cultures and traditions' – with videos of poems being read.
- You can download a free booklet from Tes with poems from other cultures – www.tes.com/teaching-resource/poems-from-different-cultures-booklet-6213200.
- Some countries have different poetic forms that you and the children might not have heard of and there is a very interesting website which explores different types of poetry in Japan, Cambodia, Vietnam, India, Russia, Latvia, Italy, Germany and Canada – www.theyellowsparrow.com/traditional-forms-of-poetry/ – with explanations and examples.

Activities

Activity 1: Translations

For this activity, you need a selection of poems in different languages. Here are some examples you could use:

Poems in Spanish – www.spanishplayground.net/spanish-poems-for-kids/
Poems in French – https://snippetsofparis.com/french-poems-kids/
Songs and rhymes by language – www.mamalisa.com/?t=el
If you want to buy some bilingual publications, there are some great examples here – https://worldkidlit.wordpress.com/2019/09/23/bilingual-poetry-for-kids/

If possible, include poems in the languages of the children in your class. If yours is a monolingual, English class, perhaps ask the children which languages they would like to explore through poetry.

Give the children access to a poem in a language other than English. This could be conducted in a number of ways: a child in your class who speaks the language could read it aloud (or their parent/sibling); you could read it if you feel confident; you could find an audio version online. Ask the children to close their eyes and listen to the poem. Do they recognise any words? Do any words sound like English words?

Show the poem written out on the board, in its original language. Does this help with making sense of the poem, when we see the words written down? Are any words similar to English? Take some time here for discussion, then put a translation on the board, in English. Read the poem in English (or ask a volunteer to do so). Ask children to work in pairs and choose six words from the poem in English and write these in a list. Then, next to these words, write the word as it appears in the other language in the poem. Children then leave their lists on their tables and take a walk around the classroom, exploring each other's lists and making a note of any words they would like to add to their own list. This raises an awareness of different languages; how they sound and how they are spelt.

Finish by listening again to the poem in a language other than English and then read the poem again in English, for a final comparison.

Activity 2: Poetry and people's lives

Tell the children they are going to start a poetry project, focusing on finding out about different poets from across the globe and reading/listening to their poems. From this research, they are going to put together a class anthology with all their favourites, alongside autobiographies of the poets, written by the pupils.

Give plenty of opportunities to access the Children's Poetry Archive – https://childrens.poetryarchive.org/explore/?type=poets. If you are working with very young children, you can choose which poets and poems are most suitable and perhaps explore one a day/week on the interactive whiteboard.

As the days/weeks go by, ask the class to start thinking about how they would like to create the anthology – audio recordings/short films/using Padlet/paper portfolios. If they are using paper or e-portfolios, how might they illustrate their chosen poems or present the lives of the poets they have selected?

Once the class anthology has been constructed, share with other classes/the whole school/a school you are twinned with and, if possible, invite parents in to share the experience.

Activity 3: Languages and list poems

List poems are fun, easy to put together and really get children to think about language (see Chapter 6 for more examples of how to use list poems). Multilingual list poems are a powerful resource in terms of enhancing your foreign language lessons, promoting language development generally and expanding children's vocabulary around particular topics. Let us imagine you are exploring the topic of different places around the world – countries and continents. Children could identify features of a range of countries:

Spain – hot and dry, beaches and mountains
Italy – lakes and mountains
Australia – vast emptiness, hot desert, stunning beaches
Nepal – snowy mountains, exotic wildlife
India – 65,000 animal species, jungles, mountains, desert

The National Geographic Kids website – https://kids.nationalgeographic.com/ – is an excellent resource where children can collect information for this project. They could then begin putting their list poems together, first in English. Here is an example:

Italy
Sky blue lakes
Snow-capped mountains

> Forested slopes
> Wildflowers galore
> Migrating birds
> Heading for Africa.
> (Virginia Bower)
>
> They could then have a go at changing some of the words into the language of the country they have chosen. It is probably best at first to just alter the nouns, as they translate easily using an online programme such as Google Translate or DeepL. Here is an example using the poem above:
>
> **Italy**
> Sky blue laghi
> Snow-capped montagne
> Forested piste
> Fiore galore
> Migrating uccelli
> Heading for Africa.
> (Virginia Bower)
>
> Imagine the wonderful poems that will emerge, using a wide range of languages, ideas and rich vocabulary – you cannot go wrong!

References

Bower, V. (2017) *Supporting Pupils with EAL in the Primary Classroom*, London: Open University Press.

Carlos, M. S., August, D., McLaughlin, B., Snow, C. E., Lippman, D. N., Lively, T. J. & White, C. E. (2004) 'Closing the Gap: Addressing the Vocabulary Needs of English Language Learners in Bilingual and Mainstream Classrooms', *Reading Research Quarterly*, 39, 2, 188–215.

Cobb, W. & Bower, V. (2022) *Language Learning and Intercultural Understanding in the Primary School*, Abingdon: Routledge.

Cummins, J. (1979) *Cognitive/Academic Language Proficiency, Linguistic Interdependence, the Optimum Age Question and Some Other Matters*, Working Papers on Bilingualism, No. 19, 121–129.

Cummins, J. (1981) 'The Role of Primary Language Development in Promoting Educational Success for Language Minority Students', in California State Department of Education (ed.), *Schooling and Language Minority Students: A Theoretical Framework*, Los Angeles: Evaluation, Dissemination and Assessment Center California State University.

Hashemi, M. R. & Gowdasiaei, F. (2005) 'An Attribute-Treatment Interaction Study: Lexical-Set versus Semantically-Unrelated Vocabulary Instruction', *RELC Journal*, 36, 3, 341–361.

The Good Schools Guide (2021) 'Speech and Language Difficulties', Available at: www.goodschoolsguide.co.uk/special-educational-needs/types-of-sen/speech-and-language. Accessed 21.12.2021.

Xiao, R. & McEnery, T. (2006) 'Collocation, Semantic Prosody, and Near Synonymy: A Cross-Linguistic Perspective', *Applied Linguistics*, 27, 1, 103–129.

6 Using poems in science and maths

This chapter puts forward the idea that poetry can be used to enhance the science and maths curricula or, in the case of the early years curriculum, the areas relating to these subjects. The importance of linking disciplines to promote a creative approach is discussed with reference to three particular elements: utility, originality and aesthetics. The chapter then examines specific examples of how poetry might be used to enhance science-related teaching and learning, including a focus on metaphor, before exploring the use of poetry within maths. The maths section examines three themes – counting, constraints and patterns.

Introduction

I would contend that the use of poems in science and maths lessons in primary classrooms is very rare! It is probably more common in early years settings, when rhymes and songs are widely used to embed learning, but there are undoubtedly areas of the early years curriculum where poems might be used more regularly as a resource and there are most certainly opportunities to be exploited for older children to use poems in these two subjects. In the powerful document, 'Guiding Principles for Learning in the Twenty-first Century' (Hughes and Acedo, 2015, p. 19), the authors state that 'Many of the world's most pressing problems are so complex that they cannot be solved from one epistemological framework: they require an interdisciplinary approach that draws from different fields'. When I read this, it resonated so tellingly with the messages I wanted to convey through the book, and particularly in this chapter. I strongly believe that if we continue to 'silo' subjects, failing to make authentic connections between disciplines, then we are failing our pupils in terms of preparing them to lead productive, fulfilled and flourishing lives, where they feel confident to address these complex, 'pressing problems' in a proactive, sustainable way.

Hughes and Acedo (2015, p. 19) identify as part of this, the imperative to promote creativity across disciplines and that this creativity has need of three essential elements: utility, originality and aesthetics. In the first section of this chapter, therefore, I discuss these three elements in relation to poetry, maths and science, before going on to examine more specific examples of how poetry might be employed in these two subjects. I hope that, as you go through this chapter, the connections between poetry, science and maths become very clear and that you feel you can use the activities presented towards the end of the chapter to enhance your pedagogies and children's experience.

DOI: 10.4324/9781003154174-7

Science, maths and poetry: utility, originality and aesthetics

Science, maths and poetry all benefit from a creative approach, an open mindedness, and a preparedness to be surprised. But what do we mean by a creative approach and how might this manifest itself as we bring these subjects together? Hughes and Acebo's (2015, p. 19) focus on what they identify as the three necessary elements of creativity seems to me to have merit in terms of how we might visualise creativity and enable us to make authentic links between disciplines. Figure 6.1 represents these ideas in diagrammatic form which

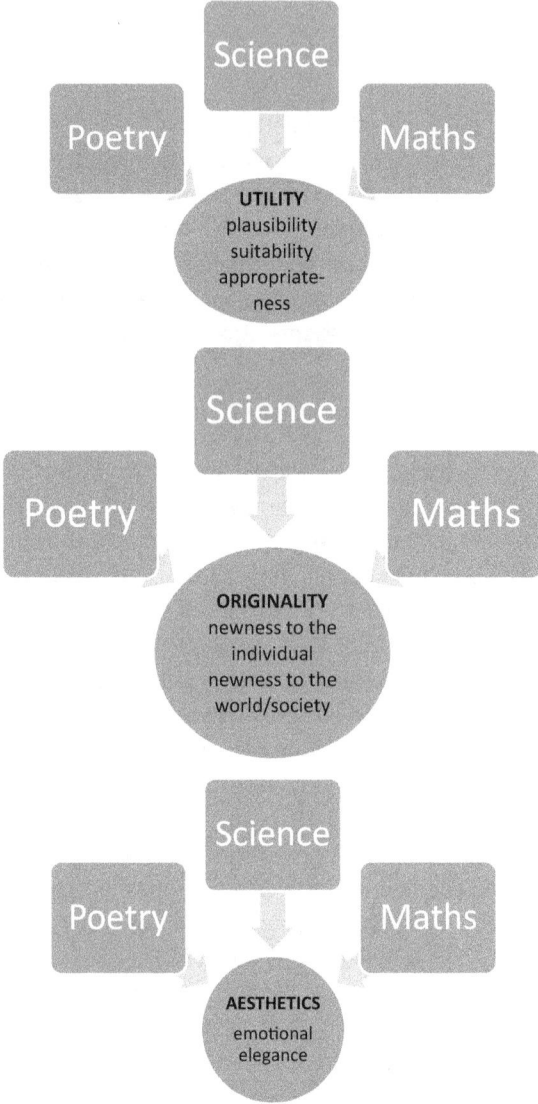

Figure 6.1 Science, maths and poetry: utility, originality and aesthetics (adapted from the ideas of Hughes and Acedo [2015, p. 16])

I hope organises the information in a way that allows for systematic consideration of these concepts and the three subjects.

Utility

Within the diagram, you will see that the authors define utility in terms of plausibility, suitability and appropriateness. To put this into context, we can be creative with our approach to a word problem in maths, perhaps using different methods to check our calculations; but these methods must be suitable and plausible and appropriate otherwise our creativity is wasted. Children might be encouraged try out their scientific hypothesis – we think the marble, when dropped, will reach the ground faster than the feather – in different ways, perhaps altering who drops the objects, from where, from what height and so on. Again, creative approaches can be encouraged but these need to be plausible, suitable and appropriate. But where does poetry fit into this?

Think for a moment of the poetic form already used in several of the chapters – the haiku. The traditional way of approaching a haiku poem is to write three lines, with the following syllabic pattern – 5-7-5. However, this can be quite constraining, and children can be encouraged to take a creative approach to this and 'bend the rules' if they wish. But what must be held in mind is that a haiku has a unique utility: to capture the essence of something in just a few words; to make us see an aspect of the world through a new lens. If, through inappropriate creativity this is lost, the haiku loses its resonance.

When these aspects regularly come to the fore during discussions and question and answer sessions, children will begin to make links between disciplines – how a creative approach to a science investigation can be influenced in the same way as we might approach the writing of a poem or the solving of a maths problem. Questions are so important here, to draw out these connections, deepen understanding and promote creativity: What if we have five lines in our haiku: what effect will this have? Why can't we use subtraction to solve this word problem?

Originality

Hughes and Acebo (2015, p.16) write that the 'creative thinker will see hidden patterns, reconceptualise the fundaments of a state of affairs, step back and see the big picture, and entertain ideas that have not been thought of before'. Children often have more ability to do this than adults, as their opinions are still forming and there is a naivety to their approach which lends itself to seeing patterns and envisaging possibilities. However, they need to be learning within an ethos that supports this and where they feel safe to investigate, experiment and suggest different ideas. Maths, science and poetry all offer opportunities for this within an open classroom culture. Encouraging children to explain how they tackled a maths investigation often results in myriad approaches that we, as adults, will not have considered. With science, children can bring their perspectives to the concept under study and these will be original in the context of your class, as the origin of their ideas will be their unique upbringing and home life. They may also be original on a wider scale – bringing a freshness to more universal scientific 'truths' – and it is likely that many scientific principles started in the minds of very young learners. Originality often emerges through freedom and when we consider poetry and the writing of poems, it is important to consider that some children will welcome this aspect of creativity; to be freed from rules and form. In Chapter 4, I discuss the pros and cons of using poetic form and the 'rules' of these can offer appropriate support for some children. However, when children are ready, greater freedom can lead to more originality.

Aesthetics

In Figure 6.1, we can see that aesthetics are defined by Hughes and Acedo as 'emotional elegance'. Now, this we might immediately attribute more easily to poetry and the way that poets take unique and creative approaches to produce this elegance. Maths and science might require more of a leap of faith, if we have not considered these subjects in this light before.

Dijkgraaf (2016), provides a useful starting point, stating that 'Maths becomes beautiful through the power and elegance of its arguments and formulae; through the bridges it builds between previously unconnected worlds'. Consider for a moment what happens when we change three words (in italics) in this quote: '*Poetry* becomes beautiful through the power and elegance of its *language* and *structure*; through the bridges it builds between previously unconnected worlds'. Not everyone will find maths formulae beautiful; nor indeed, poetry. However, when somebody draws attention to a subject in this way, we can begin to view it more through their eyes and can link how *they* feel with how we might feel about a different subject – art perhaps, or music. We might begin to notice the elegance of number patterns or the absolute beauty of leaf symmetry. There comes a realisation that so many apparently separate aspects of our lives are connected in some way, and this can bring about a sense of security and a feeling of belonging more securely to the human race. Not to mention triggering brain synapses in myriad ways. Indeed, 'scientists have found that the sight of an elegant equation activates the same part of the brain as a beautiful piece of art or music' (Science Focus, 2014) and this I am sure could also include poetry.

I want to finish this section with a powerful quote from Hughes and Acebo. I am aware that I have used their work a great deal so far in this chapter, but this was a conscious decision as I think reading their principles can have a profound effect on our thinking about pedagogy and I hope I have persuaded you to read their work yourself! Anyway, here is the quote:

> Students need to plan for a future that is likely to develop at an accelerating rate and where creativity will be as important as sustainability for the survival of the human species.
>
> (Hughes and Acebo, 2015, p. 18)

It will be useful to bear this in mind as you move onto the next sections, which focus more specifically on science and maths and their connections with poetry.

Science and poetry

Scientific concepts can be challenging to grasp and need to be introduced in a way that encourages children to hypothesise, question, discuss, argue, experiment and investigate. Interestingly, these are words which might be used when we are sharing and exploring poems with children. So, why not bring the subjects together, to enhance both? Illingworth (2015) writes that:

> there are many overlaps in the process of writing a poem or conducting an experiment. When you start off you have to follow rules and regulations that produce half-expected results. However, it is only by fully exploring these rules that you get an underlying sense of how they can be used to create your own work, or how they must be rejected in favour of a new form or hypothesis.

Drawing attention to 'overlaps' and similarities in approaches when discussing concepts with children can often bring about an understanding not achieved using other pedagogies. Hughes and Acedo (2015, p. 22) argue that it is more effective to articulate learning 'around concepts rather than topics' to promote deeper understanding and a higher level of abstraction which enables a transfer of learning between contexts and cultures, people and places. Addressing a concept through more than one discipline has the advantage of allowing principles to be applied and transferred. The observation needed, for example, for an accurate reporting of a science investigation reflects the detailed reporting of observations needed for a poem that 'speaks' to the reader.

Science, poetry and life

Scientists and poets seek to think about and find out more about life on earth and beyond and to articulate this information to their chosen audiences. They have the power to open up possibilities through their work and to make us all aware that these possibilities are infinite and that there are no easy answers. As Illingworth (2015) writes, 'Poetry and science are both just trying to make sense of the world in which we live, striving to describe nature in terms so absolute that they cannot possibly be denied'. Sam Illingworth is a lecturer in Science Communication and researches the links between science, society and cultural media. He writes what he describes as 'bad poems about good science' and, despite this self-deprecation, it is well worth taking a look at some of these. They are more appropriate for an upper Key Stage 2 class, but you might find them interesting of themselves to give *you* ideas or just to enjoy as poems. After each poem, Illingworth provides the scientific research which inspired the poem, providing another level of interest and information for you and/or your pupils. There is a very powerful example about dragonflies, which I think children would love and you can find it here: https://thepoetryofscience.scienceblog.com/2413/dragons-across-the-ocean/.

Padel (2011) believes that 'Science was born in poetry', providing examples of how, pre-Socrates, those who were attempting to answer the big questions about life, creation, the universe often addressed these in verse. Poets and scientists attempt to find a way to the essence of something and, if successful, they arrive at 'a universal insight or law through the particular' (ibid.); arriving at the 'grand and abstract' through 'precision' (ibid.). Bhatt (2016) gives the example of 18th-century science papers presented in verse because 'poetry was considered the language of intellect and the future'.

Poetry and science both 'tolerate uncertainty' (Padel, 2011) – they suggest rather than insist; pose possibilities rather than sureties; leave gaps for us to fill. Children (and indeed, adults) often want an answer – the one correct, indisputable answer – to a problem or a question, and life of course is rarely that simple. Both science and poetry teach us to manage uncertainty, uncomfortable though it may be, and demand an openness to ideas, a positive approach to problem-solving and a creative stance to finding new ways of understanding. Global issues such as climate change, sustainable development, biodiversity loss, the forced migration of vast populations and environmental disasters need to be addressed by an upcoming generation who are prepared for the excitement and challenge of 21st-century life. Both science and poetry offer us 'alternative realities' (Illingworth, 2015) which enable a consideration of how things might be rather than how things are and this of course is absolutely vital in terms of considering ways to ensure a sustainable future. There are some useful poems you might want to explore here which focus on the environment and could provide a useful catalyst for discussion – www.sciencerhymes.com.au/environmental-poetry.

Science and poetry can help us to learn more about ourselves, our identity and our place in the world and both require us to use our senses at a high level if we hope to gain the most from this use. Through this use of senses, we learn about the world, our place in it (naureenghani, 2016) and about our innermost beliefs and feelings. A powerful example of how poetry and science, feelings and observations might be brought together is in the poem, 'Quiet Night Thought' by Tang Dynasty poet Li Bai:

> Before my bed there's a pool of light
> I wonder if it's frost on the ground
> Looking up, I find the moon bright
> Then bowing my head, I drown in homesickness

> *Chuáng qián míngyuè guāng*
> *Yí shì dìshang shuāng*
> *Jǔtóu wàng míngyuè*
> *D-tóu sī gùxiāng*

> 床前明月光
> 疑是地上霜
> 舉頭望明月
> 低頭思故鄉

From a poetry criticism perspective, this has such beautiful imagery and use of metaphor: 'pool of light' and 'drown in homesickness'. If we were to use the poem to consider our own thoughts and feelings, it is the ideal starting point for a discussion about belonging, loneliness, community and so forth. Bringing in the science element, we could ask children what they think about the words 'pool of light'. Surely it is water that is normally associated with a pool? Why has the poet used this here? This could lead to discussions about reflections, beams of light and so on. Why did the poet think it might be frost on the ground? How is this similar to light? What kind of moon would there need to be to provide a 'pool of light'? You can hopefully begin to see how we can weave aspects of science, poetry and life together in this example. The next section looks in more depth about how we might use metaphor to enhance children's learning experience.

Metaphor in science and poetry

One of the key similarities that Padel (2011) identifies between science and poetry is the use of metaphor; allowing us to see the familiar through a new lens and helping to make the unfamiliar less strange. Sfard (1998, p. 4) describes this as 'conceptual osmosis between everyday and scientific discourses, letting our primary intuition shape scientific ideas and the formal conceptions feed back into the intuition'. Metaphor also allows us to make clear to others, ideas which might otherwise not be grasped, by comparing to something that is more manageable and digestible. With science, being able to imagine that, because something exists in a particular form then it might well exist in another, can be confirmed through metaphor (Bhatt, 2016) and in this way, a scientific concept moves forward. Poems provide a bridge here, as the use of metaphor is an accepted practice and, once recognised and appreciated, this understanding can be applied to other areas of the curriculum.

Following on from the moon theme in the previous section, this poem by T.E Hulme could be shared with children of all ages and is powerful in its use of simile and metaphor:

Autumn
A touch of cold in the Autumn night –
I walked abroad,
And saw the ruddy moon lean over a hedge
Like a red-faced farmer.
I did not stop to speak, but nodded,
And round about were the wistful stars
With white faces like town children.

There is a great deal to be enjoyed with this poem and so much to explore. The powerful use of minimal vocabulary – a 'touch of cold', the 'wistful stars' – could lead to powerful discussion with children. In terms of science, the moon, stars, sun, planets and so on are explored in different areas of the curriculum and children often have a natural fascination with earth and space which can be exploited for projects, homework, holiday portfolios and so on. The Year 5 curriculum specifically identifies 'Earth and Space' as a topic and this poem might be used here as an introduction; perhaps asking the question, 'Why does the moon appear to us in different phases or different colours?' 'Why does the moon sometimes appear much closer than other times?' You certainly do not need to know the answer to all the questions the children will ask; it is about setting them the task to research, investigate and report back. A poem such as Hulme's can be the catalyst for this type of investigation, leading to deeper and more meaningful learning, and connections across the curriculum with English and the use of imagery for particular effects. But, perhaps more importantly, it contains metaphors which demand a stretch of the imagination – something much needed in science when we begin to consider the 'big questions' about life.

Maths and poetry

One of the interesting connections between poetry and maths is that many students fear them! Often both children and adults will say 'I can't do maths' or 'I haven't got a maths brain' or 'I just don't get poetry'. Brooks (no date) says that, for her, maths is always a 'cardio workout' in that it causes so much stress and a much-raised heartbeat. She uses poetry to enable her to engage more positively with maths and says that 'poetry can introduce us to this idea of trial and error' – much needed in the solving of maths problems for example – and can act as an effective counterpoint to the central tenet of maths – that there is a right and a wrong answer. If you are interested in this idea, you might want to watch the whole of Brooks' TEDx talk – www.youtube.com/watch?v=nGkfRN2i6vY&t=1059s.

As Brooks suggests, the root of maths and/or poetry anxiety might well originate in early experiences of these subjects that have not been positive, and these deep-rooted memories are difficult to overcome. We may well agree with these sentiments ourselves, but for us as classroom practitioners, there is no escape! We cannot permit ourselves to pass on our feelings about more or less favoured subjects; our duty is to give children the very best experience of every subject and, where possible, to allow them to bring to the subject what they already know and enjoy. One way to 'dismantle the fear' (STEM and NGSS, 2020) is to link the two subjects together and this is the aim of this section – to provide ideas and ways that you can combine poetry and maths to ensure a more innovative approach and to dispel any existing fears. To get you started, you might want to visit JoAnne Growney's blog where she provides some examples of one sentence poems about maths – https://poetrywithmathematics.blogspot.com/2021/12/one-sentence-poems.html. Within this blog, there is an amusing poem by Brian McCabe entitled 'Two Quadrilaterals' which older children would very much enjoy – https://poetrywithmathematics.blogspot.com/2021/12/stories-of-quadrilaterals.html#more. There are also links to JoAnne on Twitter and her full website.

The article from STEM and NGSS focusses on how to see maths in poetry. The authors suggest three links – counting, constraint and patterns – and the following sections will explore these, with examples of how these ideas can be explored in the classroom to link maths and poetry.

Counting

The STEM and NGSS article points out that poetry was traditionally an oral art form and much depended on the way poems were recited in terms of the rhythm, the rise and fall, the prosody, the stress and intonation. To achieve this, a focus is required on syllable use, numbers of words used (if we think about the examples of haiku poems I have used in Chapters 1 and 4), line length, length and number of stanzas and so forth. In the article, it is noted that 'the numerical features of math provide skeletal structure to the "flesh and blood" that is the poetry' (STEM and NGSS, 2020), and it is suggested that an approach to a poem – when we are exploring how it is constructed – could be through counting, making it more accessible to young learners. Let us take the following wonderful poem as an example:

Flint
An emerald is as green as grass,

> A ruby red as blood;
> A sapphire shines as blue as heaven;
> A flint lies in the mud.
>
> A diamond is a brilliant stone,
> To catch the world's desire;
> An opal holds a fiery spark;
> But a flint holds fire.
> (Christina Rossetti)

Children could start by doing a counting investigation:

- How many stanzas are there?
- How many lines in each stanza?
- How many syllables in each line?

This could be followed by a further investigation, deepening the learning and encouraging critical thinking, whereby you change the questions slightly:

- Why are there only two stanzas?
- Why are there four lines in each stanza?
- Why is there a regular pattern of syllables?
- Why does this change with the final line?

As the questions become more focused on 'Why?' the degree of challenges increases. Whilst there is still a focus on numbers, we are asking children to explore what lies behind the numbers and what has led the poet to take this approach. Earlier in the chapter I mentioned the excellent 'Guiding Principles' document written by Hughes and Acedo (2015). In this text, the authors write that children's conceptual understanding needs to go through a series of stages, if they are to see how individual pieces of information 'fit' into the bigger picture. These are the stages, which I have adapted and linked with the poem above:

- Identifying and knowing about separate pieces of information – the poem has two stanzas, with four lines in each. The syllables go eight, six, eight, six, eight, six, eight, five. The poem compares precious stones with flint.
- Organising information into groups – the way the poem is presented, with specific numbers of lines and stanzas – allows for comparisons between objects, leading to a powerful denouement.
- Linking ideas within and across topics – the way that ideas are expressed, with specific numbers of syllables in each line, leads the reader through the ideas in a powerful way.
- Generalising ideas to form a set of principles – there are mathematical and life principles here. With maths, an awareness that line and stanza length has a considerable impact on how a poem is received. With life principles, it is about finding beauty in the ordinary.
- Create broad statements about the topic – this would be an interesting challenge to set children. Could they produce broad statements about this poem; some with a mathematical focus and others about the poem content?

Constraint

In Chapter 4, I discuss how, with poetry, we can break the rules of writing to suit our purpose. However, of course certain poetic forms do have very clear rules, for example a sonnet has 14 lines, rhyming couplets are two lines which must rhyme, haiku poems generally have 17 syllables. The links here to maths are clear and it is the counting of the syllables or lines or stanzas and the conforming to the required structure which makes the poem what it is. Of course, *content* will change – it could be one of Shakespeare's 154 sonnets which cover universal themes such as love, death and jealousy, or the rhyming stanzas you can find in Andreae and Parker-Rees' 'Giraffes Can't Dance' (Orchard Books, 1999) – but the mathematical qualities and constraints remain and drawing attention to these can be another way to lure children into the magic of maths and poetry.

For some children, the constraints of particular poetic forms can be very reassuring; they enjoy the boundaries imposed and feel more comfortable writing themselves within these boundaries. For others, the constraints are less welcome and I discuss this further in Chapter 4 when considering the use of form. In the same way, the constraints of having to undertake a mathematical calculation in a particular way can be supportive for some children, as they work through in a systematic and ordered way. For others, who see the mathematical patterns more naturally, having to adopt a specific approach when their own way of approaching the calculation seems more fitting can be frustrating and de-motivating. Interdisciplinary discussions about aspects of learning such as these can help children better understand how *they* learn, how *others* learn and how there is rarely one way to approach a piece of learning or a task. Life lessons indeed! There is a powerful TEDx talk by Dr Patrick Bahls which you might enjoy watching, entitled 'Math and Poetry: A Terrifying and Terrific Combination' where he focuses primarily on constraints. You can find the video here – www.youtube.com/watch?v=-MSMhnR-WSM.

Patterns

Patterns is a wonderful theme to have for a topic with any year group. I would argue that every subject of the curriculum could be explored through patterns, but I will just look at maths and poetry here (you might want to consider how you could bring other subjects into your planning for this topic). We often ask children to find patterns in maths and there is specific mention of patterns in Development Matters (26 references) and the maths programmes of study for Key Stage 1 and 2 (eight references). Of course, poetry is very much defined by patterns, relating to stanzas, line length, rhyme and so forth. There is a wonderful quote on the Poetry Teatime blog, where Brave Writer says:

> Poetry is like a spiderweb: every thread (or word or line) is carefully connected with the threads (and words and lines) around it. The poet constructs the poem so that all the lines and words come together to form an eye-catching pattern for you to enjoy.
>
> (Brave Writer, no date)

This is a great blog post and worth a read. The author gives examples of 'patterns of the eye' and 'patterns of the ear' with useful ways to explore patterns in poems.

Using poems in science and maths

Drawing attention to patterns – with symmetry for example – can be another way of making powerful connections for children. They might be exploring symmetry in 2-D and 3-D shapes and then realise that there is a certain pattern and symmetry in a poem you share with them in terms of the rhyming scheme. If we look at Judith Nicholls' poem 'Winter' which you can find here – https://childrens.poetryarchive.org/poem/winter/ – there is a very powerful rhyming scheme, creating a pattern for each stanza and this pattern makes us read the poem in a particular way. The pattern and rhyme add to the impact of the words, in the same way that the beauty of mathematical symmetry in a piece of architecture delivers the impact intended by the designer. The potential to find and use patterns across the curriculum is enormous and I hope this has given you some food for thought.

Activities – maths

Activity 1: Numbers and counting

The most obvious use for poems in maths is with children in the early years when they are learning numbers and counting. Having rhymes and songs can enable children to hear the same words and sounds over and over and there are often opportunities for them to make up their own versions whilst retaining the number order.

Here is an example that might be useful for younger children:

> One, two, kittens that mew
> Two, three, birds on a tree
> Three, four, shells on the shore,
> Four, five, bees from the hive,
> Five, six, the cow that licks,
> Six, seven, rooks in the heaven,
> Seven, eight, sheep at the gate,
> Eight, nine, clothes on a line,
> Nine, ten, the little black hen.
>
> (Anon.)

This poem would be perfect as the basis of a display, with children creating collages for each of the lines, showing the actions or creatures or objects. As a class, you could create your own version, replacing the nouns with children's ideas, inevitably leading to a discussion about which words would be suitable, in order to keep the pattern and rhyme scheme consistent.

Another useful example is the poem 'Mice and Cat' by Clive Sansom – www.poemhunter.com/clive-sansom/poems/. Although this poem only counts to four, there is plenty of scope for children to think of their own extra stanzas which would incorporate numbers to ten. Here is an example I wrote:

> Five mice, six mice
> Sniffing at the plate
> Crumbs for them both
> Plus seven and eight

80   *Using poems in science and maths*

Activity 2: Ordinal numbers

Apart from linking to the date, it might be difficult to think of useful, interesting and relevant ways to develop children's understanding and accurate use of ordinal numbers. Having poems which include ordinal numbers can be a useful approach. Here is a fun example:

> I went fishing,
> Took some bait.
> Didn't go early,
> Didn't go late.
> Caught eight fishes
> To put in my pail
> Seven were mackerel,
> But the eighth was a whale.
>
> The seven were easy
> To put into the tin,
> But that whale caused me trouble
> Before I packed him in!
>
> Took my catch home.
> What did Mother say?
> 'Get those eight fish out of here –
> We're having steak today!'
>   (Anon.)

Although the poem only makes explicit reference to one ordinal number – eighth, you could replace the numbers so that the ordinal number changes, for example 'Six were mackerel, but the seventh was a whale'.

Activities – science

Activity 3: Using kennings

I always think that kenning poems lend themselves to subjects like science in a very useful way. A kenning is a compound metaphorical phrase (usually two words) to describe something – for example, a house might be a 'shelter-provider', or a squirrel could be a 'tree climber'. Kennings originated in Old English and Norse poetry – in Old Norse, 'kenna' means 'to know, perceive'. The potential with kenning poems is that children get to know and perceive aspects of science and find words to describe these, using these concise, compound phrases. Although simple in structure, these poems need a strong knowledge of a topic and a good understanding of associated terminology and are therefore powerful constructions to support all children and specifically children with English as an additional language.

Imagine you are teaching Year 2 science, with the topic of habitats and the plants and animals in different habitats. Children could work in groups to create lists of different habitats (lexical sets – lists of words on a particular subject – were discussed in Chapter 5, if you remember). Choose one of the habitats and ask them to devise another list with words that describe the habitat. For example, they might choose desert as a habitat and the following words might emerge: 'sandy', 'hot', 'uninhabited', 'dry', 'vast', 'parched', 'oasis', 'drought', 'barren', 'cactus', 'dunes', 'endless', 'rocky', 'scorched', 'wild'. Really push them with this part of the activity, offering words they may not have heard of, using images to provoke more ideas. This collection of a lexicon associated with a topic is an essential aspect of all subjects. Here, they are thinking of habitats and science but of course they may go on to use these words in stories, non-fiction writing, geography lessons and so forth. They are building a vocabulary for life, so take time with this.

Now explain that they are going to create a kenning poem and that it is to read as a riddle or a word game – describing the desert without mentioning the word and then setting it for others to guess the subject. Give them an example:

The Desert
Sand dunes forever
Scorching heat
Vast emptiness
Parched plants
Deep roots
Water searching
Rocky soil
A wild beauty
(Virginia Bower)

Children could then work individually or in pairs or small groups, creating their own kennings and then 'testing' their friends. This could also be completed as a class activity with younger children.

Activity 4: Our wonderful world

Walter de la Mare's poem 'The Rainbow' is a wonderful resource to use to explore natural phenomena. Most of us find rainbows delightful and somewhat mysterious. I recently saw a completely vertical rainbow, which seemed to meet the ground just in front of where I was driving my car. It was completely mesmerising, and these moments bring to the fore the world's wonders for which it can sometimes be difficult to find words. Walter de la Mare's poem captures the essence of a rainbow in the most beautiful way:

> **The Rainbow**
> I saw the lovely arch
> Of Rainbow span the sky,
> The gold sun burning
> As the rain swept by.
>
> In bright-ringed solitude
> The showery foliage shone
> One lovely moment,
> And the Bow was gone.
>
> Changing weather patterns, making scientific observations, using scientific language, examining light refraction, gathering data – these are all skills developed across the science curriculum and, in the early years, within the specific learning area of Understanding the World. Having a poem to start off a conversation about the natural phenomenon that is a rainbow, would be a creative approach to this topic. There is a useful page on the National Geographic website which discusses rainbows and here is an extract:
>
>> Viewers on the ground can only see the light reflected by raindrops above the horizon. Because each person's horizon is a little different, no one actually sees a full rainbow from the ground. In fact, no one sees the same rainbow – each person has a different antisolar point, each person has a different horizon. Someone who appears below or near the 'end' of a rainbow to one viewer will see another rainbow, extending from his or her own horizon.
>>
>> (National Geographic, no date)
>
> Imagine the incredible discussions that are likely to emerge from the use of these two texts – the poem and the website extract (there is also an example of a painting activity using rainbows and this same poem in Chapter 9). An activity such as this has the potential to bring together the three aspects of creativity mentioned earlier in the chapter – utility, originality and aesthetics – and to provoke a depth of memorable learning in children of any age.

References

Bhatt, Z. (2016) 'The love affair between science and poetry', The New Statesman, Available at: www.newstatesman.com/culture/2016/06/love-affair-between-science-and-poetry. Accessed on 17.12.2021.

Brave Writer (no date) 'Poetry prompt: Patterns', Available at: https://poetryteatime.com/blog/poetry-prompt-patterns. Accessed on 26.01.2022.

Brooks, L. (no date) 'Poetry: A Simple Solution to Math Anxiety', Available at: www.youtube.com/watch?v=nGkfRN2i6vY. Accessed 17.12.2021.

Dijkgraaf, R. (2016) 'Magic Numbers: Can Maths Equations Be Beautiful?' The Guardian, Available at: www.theguardian.com/science/2016/nov/21/magic-numbers-can-maths-equations-be-beautiful. Accessed on 23.01.2022.

Dork, C. (2012) 'Why Poets Sometimes Think in Numbers', Available at: http://talkingwriting.com/why-poets-sometimes-think-in-numbers. Accessed 21.06.2021.

Hughes. C. & Acedo, C. (2015) *Guiding Principles for Learning in the Twenty-first Century*, Brussels: International Academy of Education.

Illingworth, S. (2015) 'Science vs. Poetry', *PLOS*, Available at: https://scicomm.plos.org/2015/11/09/science-vs-poetry-by-sam-illingworth/. Accessed 18.12.2021.

National Geographic (no date) *Rainbow*, Available at: https://tinyurl.com/2p9922rx. Accessed on 26.01.2022.

naureenghani (2016) 'Mind and Matter: The Intersection of Poetry and Science', *PLOS*, Available at: https://ecrcommunity.plos.org/2016/01/15/mind-and-matter-the-intersection-of-poetry-and-science/. Accessed 18.12.2021.

Padel, R. (2011) 'The Science of Poetry, the Poetry of Science', *The Guardian*, Available at: www.theguardian.com/books/2011/dec/09/ruth-padel-science-poetry. Accessed 17.12.2021.

Science Focus (2014) *Can Maths be Beautiful?*, Available at: www.sciencefocus.com/science/can-maths-be-beautiful/. Accessed on 24.01.2022.

Sfard, A. (1998) 'On Two Metaphors for Learning and the Dangers of Choosing Just One', *Educational Researcher*, 27, 2, 4-13.

STEM and NGSS (2020) 'STEM Series: Discovering Math in Poetry', Available at: www.acornnaturalists.com/blog/stem-poetry/. Accessed 17.12.2021.

7 Poems for times and spaces

The key focus of this chapter is how poetry can enable a better understanding of the world in which we live – past, present and future – with the early years curriculum held up as an exemplar. There is a section focusing on how significant issues, with an historical or geographical focus, might be explored by poetry. This is followed by a discussion relating to the use of poetry to learn about people and events in history, and then a geography focus suggesting how geographic enquiry might be enhanced through poems.

Introduction

This chapter focuses on how poetry might be used across the subjects of history and geography or, in the case of early years, Understanding the World. Whether these areas of learning are taught discretely or as part of a general 'topic' approach in your setting, there are so many ways to use poetry to enhance your pedagogy. Lewis (no date) provides three very valid reasons for making connections between poetry and different disciplines, saying that poetry brings a 'human connection' to any subject and inserts images in the readers'/listeners' minds which means they are more likely to remember what they have learnt. He reiterates, as I do earlier in the book, that the more manageable length of many poems and the often humorous or quirky presentation of information, also helps to make curriculum subject concepts more accessible. Lewis' third point – considered by him as the most important – is the means by which poems can address challenging issues in a way that other genres cannot – 'stepping beyond the facts' and speaking to learners in powerful ways that help them to realise their own local and global significance; that what they think, say and do really matters.

These are key points and relate well to subjects such as history, geography and promoting a better understanding of the world in which we live – past, present and future. However, to make useful and powerful connections, it is important to know your curriculum well so that you can begin to look out for appropriate poems to use at times which will ensure maximum impact. Having a deep understanding of the expectations also allows you to transform what might be fairly dry, unimaginative objectives into exciting, child-centred lessons which build on children's existing knowledge of the world. The chapter begins therefore by providing an extract from the early years curriculum, to illustrate how a more creative approach might be taken, whatever key stage you teach. I then move on to examine how significant issues,

DOI: 10.4324/9781003154174-8

with an historical or geographical focus, might be explored through poetry. This is followed by a specific section exploring the use of poetry to learn about people and events in history, and then a geography focus suggesting how geographic enquiry might be enhanced through poems. The chapter ends with two practical activities for each subject, all of which could be adapted for any aged children as they go about understanding their world.

Curriculum transformation

Arguably, learning about our history and thinking about our future, understanding the world we inhabit and how best to ensure its continuation and the flourishing of life forms are the most important aspects of education – whatever age the children. What we must avoid is an atomistic approach to these areas, where prescribed objectives are ticked off and connections fail to be made with children's own lives. Instead, we need to take hold of the curriculum and transform it to suit our unique pupils and to ignite a passion within them for local, national and global concerns. Alexander (2009, p. 8) suggests that a curriculum undergoes 'a series of translations, transpositions and transformations', as teachers respond to it according to their own and their school's interpretation and adapt and change to meet the needs of their pupils. This is both normal and necessary, but it is about considering the most effective ways to transform the curriculum to gain the best results.

Development Matters (DfE, 2021, p. 100) provides a valuable overview of each of the areas of learning, and the summary of 'Understanding the World' provides a useful foundation on which we can build curricula, whatever age children we teach:

> Understanding the world involves guiding children to make sense of their physical world and their community. The frequency and range of children's personal experiences increases their knowledge and sense of the world around them – from visiting parks, libraries and museums to meeting important members of society such as police officers, nurses and firefighters. In addition, listening to a broad selection of stories, non-fiction, rhymes and poems will foster their understanding of our culturally, socially, technologically and ecologically diverse world. As well as building important knowledge, this extends their familiarity with words that support understanding across domains. Enriching and widening children's vocabulary will support later reading comprehension.

I very much appreciate this definition and find it more useful and relevant to our ever-changing world than the more prescriptive objectives outlined for Key Stage 1 and 2, which have an unfortunate leaning towards learning facts – names of countries, continents, oceans and mountain ranges for example. There is nothing wrong with this of course, providing children's learning does not stop there. The early years – as ever – lead the way on opening the door for creativity, innovation, culturally relevant teaching and recognising and celebrating the incredible diversity of the world in which we live. This, of course, lends itself quite beautifully to the use of poetry and, indeed, poems are specifically mentioned above. There is particular reference to building up familiarity with vocabulary which will have relevance for children across learning areas, enabling them to make connections. Poems are of course ideal for this, being versatile, language-focused, full of variety and range from the easily accessible and humorous, to poems which challenge and 'enable children to make senses of their physical world and their community' (ibid.).

A mechanistic approach to teaching geography and history will have a long-standing negative impact on the future generation's approach to local and global concerns. As ever, as teachers, we have a considerable responsibility to ensure we promote an awareness of these concerns, and it is never too early to begin this. A sensitive, informed approach, using creative and innovative pedagogies has the potential to spark our children's interest and bring about an awareness of their place in the world and the power they have to make changes. The next sections will discuss how we might go about this.

Addressing significant issues through poetry

Geography and history/Understanding the World are arguably the most important subjects within the curriculum in terms of producing thoughtful, responsible citizens who understand their role in the world. From early years through to Key Stage 2, there are some truly significant issues that can be connected and addressed in a way that makes them a prominent aspect of the classroom and the discussions you want to be occurring. Education for sustainable development (ESD) is an ideal example, which acknowledges and builds on the past, works hard on creating a present that is inclusive, proactive, thoughtful and respectful of environments and the species that inhabit them, and looks towards a future which enables us to flourish and cherish the planet. The Sustainable Development Goals (United Nations, 2015) were set to meet the challenges faced in the 21st century, but Warwick (2016, p. 408) believes that, in order for the 2030 deadline to be met, there is required 'nothing short of a compassionate societal transformation' and that this starts in educational contexts by 'empowering and mobilising youth' (UNESCO, 2014, p. 22).

Warwick et al. identify three dimensions of what they call 'a pedagogy of hope, with compassion and creativity at its heart' (Warwick, Warwick and Nash, 2017, p. 28). The first is 'an active concern for the common good' which 'encompasses people and the environment' (Warwick, 2016, p. 408). This requires the development of competencies to allow learners to see connections between and within systems. The second relates to place – local and global – and building an ability to understand that 'our lives today are caught up in networks of mutuality and interconnectivity' (ibid., p. 409) and that we are all part of and responsible for both our local communities and the global. The third dimension put forward by Warwick relates to time; 'inviting learners to consider the well-being needs of future generations and landscapes as well as in the present' (ibid., p. 409). This requires young learners to look back at the influences of the past, consider the implications of what is happening in the present and work towards re-envisioning a sustainable future. When we consider Warwick's dimensions, it is very clear how our history and geography curricula have the potential to truly make a difference to children's thinking and capability to respond; going far beyond the learning of facts suggested by a former education minister (BBC, 2011).

ESD requires us to open our minds to possibilities and to acknowledge that our perspectives, opinions, biases and perceptions of people and places different to our own norms, will influence the degree to which we are able to do this. Andreotti (2013, p. 12) has a wonderful phrase that helps to approach this, when she refers to 'travelling with minds'.

She argues that what we learn and how we respond to others is always influenced by our own backgrounds, experiences, culture and so on, and she uses a metaphor of travelling and four potential dispositions we might adopt. The first is where this metaphorical travelling fails to occur as a result of what Andreotti describes as the 'fenced house' mentality. Within this disposition, we tend to take a defensive position, feeling ourselves under attack for some reason. We might, in our current times, connect this with Brexit, the Covid-19 pandemic and the perceived threat from, what the tabloids have described as terms such as 'Migrant Chaos' and a '40% surge in ethnic numbers'. It is all too easy for young minds to be influenced by media hype and, through poetry they can gain an insight into more compassionate and measured observations. There is a wonderful poem read by Vanessa Kisuule here – www.bbc.com/news/av/36300602 – called 'The Magic of Childhood', written for migrant children (but of course relevant for all children), with powerful illustrations. You can also find a whole range of poems about immigration that you might want to use at this website – https://poets.org/text/immigration-poems-kids. The 'fenced house' disposition is not just about attitudes to migrants of course, but much about human life emerges from discussions on this subject and a pedagogy of hope and compassion could start here, challenging our fences and barriers.

Andreotti's second disposition is the 'caravan', reflecting a state where we are happy to look outside our own frame of reference, providing we can remain safely shielded in our perceived safe environment. In terms of ESD, this might involve an interest in people and places outside our regular existence, but without the impetus to do anything more proactive. To promote a more activist stance, children might benefit from listening to the ideas of children around the world, expressed through their poems and there are plenty to access at this UNICEF site – www.unicef.org/children-under-attack/poems-for-peace. Hearing others voicing concerns similar to their own can lead children to thinking about how they might have an influencing voice – both local and global. Warwick (2016, p. 410) demonstrated this in his Future Leaders Programme, where he worked with children between the ages of seven and 19 on sustainability projects. He describes how the children were supported to go from 'compassionate conversation' to 'compassionate enquiry' to 'compassionate action'. The pupils engaged in projects such as developing a walking bus scheme to cut down on air pollution, developing artwork to celebrate cultural diversity and promote community cohesion, and raising funds for play equipment for street children in Argentina. These projects move children from the 'caravan' disposition to the 'tent' and beyond – ideas which I will now explore.

Andreotti moves on to the third disposition for which she uses the 'tent', where we are now stepping outside our comfort zone, entering a more social community perhaps inviting others into our tent. There are more attempts to make sense of others' perspectives – fitting these into our own beliefs and recognising the diversity beyond our own experiences. To move children towards this, links might be made between settings in different counties or countries or continents, through poems, to create what I term a 'path of poetry'. Here, children share poems from poets within *their* cultures (and, hopefully, poems they have written themselves), with fellow pupils in other contexts.

Andreotti's final disposition – the 'backpack' – is worth quoting in full, as it provides a powerful metaphor for what we are trying to achieve and perhaps can promote through poetry:

> The backpack disposition indicates that we are prepared to be 'disarmed': to sleep in the rain if necessary. In this disposition, we are also willing to face the difficulties and joys of engaging with different worlds that we know will be messy and beyond the possibility of complete understanding (after all, no single frame of reference can be definite). We carry our frames of reference on our back because they help us to learn from them (i.e. from our responses to things), and they do not prevent us from being exposed to the world and taught by what is unexpected and unintelligible. This disposition requires an attitude of attentiveness, of being present and of reverence for 'being taught' – something that may seem counterintuitive to the direction our formal schooling has taken us in (by focusing as it does on compliance, 'safety', certain knowledge, tests and so on).
>
> (ibid., p. 13)

Andreotti writes that it is not about having to achieve the backpack disposition all the time – it is about working with children on *all* the dispositions and deciding when each of them is appropriate or recognising when they are being used in ways that are damaging to others or the environment. Poems can help us to expand our frames of reference and can bring uncertainty and discomfort as we attempt to find meaning in opacity. Reading and writing poems are safe activities in which to explore and leave ourselves open to new ideas. Curriculum areas such as geography and history are the ideal spaces for children to don their backpacks and take a step into the unknown.

Exploring historical events and people through poetry

There is always much debate around how curriculum subjects should be planned, delivered and assessed, in terms of the pedagogies employed and the role we allocate to the children. This debate often centres around 'Facts v Skills' (Garner and Pickford, 2021) and is never more pertinent than with the subject of history. The argument revolves around whether children should be taught certain historical facts (problematic of course in terms of which facts are chosen, by whom, and why they have been selected) or if there should be more of a skills-based approach which promotes children's exploration, investigation and engagement with sources and first-hand evidence (Tony Pickford provides a very useful overview of how the approach to the primary history curriculum has changed over the decades in his chapter in the 'Debates in Primary Education' text).

Although the latest iteration of the English National Curriculum (DfE, 2014) is weighted heavily towards delivering facts, there is evidence to suggest that teachers are also ensuring that children have the essential skills to be able to benefit from and enjoy the potential of this subject. One way of keeping a balance is to explore history through poems, enabling children to learn about key events and people, whilst using a range of skills which bring together these disciplines to deepen understanding. Lewis (no date) writes:

> There are many ways to provide students with a memorable context for your content area of study. Reading aloud part of a diary entry, letters written by soldiers to family and friends, a short story, a historical novel, an essay, a newspaper article, or a poem can help students imagine and visualize the information to be learned.

This 'memorable context' is so important if we want children to make the links essential for meaningful learning which goes beyond the memorisation of 'facts'. There are many poems available which foreground historical events or people from different eras. Some of these are written to be humorous and light-hearted; others have a more serious message to impart. Some have been written into our childhoods, associated with celebrated dates; a classic example being 'Remember, remember the 5th of November':

> Remember, remember the Fifth of November,
> The Gunpowder Treason and Plot,
> I know of no reason
> Why the Gunpowder Treason
> Should ever be forgot.
> Guy Fawkes, Guy Fawkes, t'was his intent
> To blow up the King and Parli'ment.
> Three-score barrels of powder belowTo prove old England's overthrow;
> By God's providence he was catch'd
> With a dark lantern and burning match.
> Holla boys, Holla boys, let the bells ring.
> Holloa boys, holloa boys, God save the King!
> And what should we do with him? Burn him!

This poem has all the elements to make it memorable – rhythm, rhyme, exciting content and it makes for a great choral poem with all children being involved. As a starting point for some research into this era or as the central element of a display perhaps, this poem is likely to engage your pupils. For older children, if you were teaching about explorers and oceans and continents of the world, you could use Ogden Nash's poem about Columbus – www.poemhunter.com/poem/columbus/. This is a witty, humorous poem with clever use of language. It might take some discussions with your pupils, to untangle some of the vocabulary and witticisms, but it would certainly serve as a starting point for research into this particular figure in history.

What might not be clear to children is that for centuries history has been passed down through poetry; that poetry has played a significant role in recording key events and the deeds of people – famous, infamous and obscure. This realisation can lend more significance to the genre and hopefully enable children to appreciate that poetry is part of their lives and can contribute to their understanding of the past, present and future. Osbey (2013) gives examples of the African hunting poems and the lyrical poetry of indigenous peoples 'all of which tell such a great deal about ancient sub-Saharan African social and political life, religion, mythology and warfare'. In an interview with Noam Scheindlin, Osbey goes on to write:

> The teachings of Lao-Tsu come to us in verse. Much of the accepted history of Western antiquity comes to us from Homer. And, of course, the Nahuatl philosopher-poet-king and master craftsman Nezahualcoyotl recorded in poems and songs much of what we've come to understand about life in the pre-Columbian Americas. Indeed, much if not most of what we know (or claim to know) about the ancient worlds of Africa, Asia, the Americas and Europe, we know through poetry anyway. What ancient societies can

we claim to know that didn't have generations of peripatetic bards carrying news and history in some combination of song, lyric and narrative poem?

What a powerful message this is for our young learners – that much of what we understand about the history of our own country and more globally, has been passed down through the centuries through verse. How do they feel about recording aspects of their own and their families' histories through poems, so that they add to the rich mosaic of poems handed down through the ages? This approach to history makes it real for the children we teach, and they can begin to recognise that we are all part of history being made. When you reach the activities towards the end of the chapter, Activity 1 provides an example of how you might explore this further with your pupils.

Alongside reading and listening to poems, a better understanding of aspects of history can be achieved through children writing their own. Lederle (2012) describes the idea of 'found poetry' which promotes an understanding of aspects of history, through the writing of poems. The idea is that children explore primary sources around an event or a person of historical significance – these might be photographs, letters, diaries, official documents and so on – and they gather words that they find interesting within these sources or, in the case of images, the words they inspire. They then use these words to create a poem which expresses the key idea or story revealed by the sources. You can find some very useful primary historical resources here – www.history.org.uk/primary/module/8754/primary-history-articles-for-the-school-history-su/9919/resources (you need to join the Historical Association to gain the free resources and perhaps this would be something your school might sign up to). There are plenty of free resources at the National Archives site – www.nationalarchives.gov.uk/education/ – or on an American site here – www.loc.gov/programs/teachers/getting-started-with-primary-sources/.

There are so many levels of learning occurring here with this 'found poetry' activity. Children are accessing trustworthy, robust sources of evidence; they are taking on the role of historians; they are having to synthesise and summarise information, identify key information and vocabulary and turn their findings into a completely different genre. These are not skills that they can just adopt without support. It would be useful to model the whole process, over a series of lessons perhaps, and then give them the freedom to explore, maybe working in pairs so that they can support each other. Time is needed for this activity and sessions could be spread over several weeks – perhaps a whole term – with linked homework activities and involving parents where possible. This may seem daunting but take it a step at a time and the level of learning will be quite astounding. Activity 2 towards the end of the chapter explains how you might approach this challenge.

Geographical enquiry through poetry

Geography is an all-encompassing subject in that it is essentially about gaining a better understanding of the world in which we live. This includes the people, places, environments, weather patterns, geographical features. It involves questioning, investigating, comparing and researching and in this way has significant links with 'various sciences and disciplines' (Garner and Pickford, 2021, p. 187). Garner writes that geography 'is seen as bridging the gap between arts and sciences', and if we think of it in this way there is the potential for powerful links to be made across curriculum subjects and bringing in poetry to enhance our pedagogies. Kirman (2007, p. 207) sums this up wonderfully when he writes, 'Geography is an obvious subject for poetry since everything has to happen someplace'.

In the same way as history, geography as a subject has undergone much scrutiny of its pedagogies through the 20th century and into the 21st and the whole 'Facts v Skills' debate raises its head again. With a subject which encompasses a vast area – literally and metaphorically – there is always a temptation to reduce it down to measurable, assessable components and to deliver these components to pupils in bite-size chunks of information. A rigid, facts-based approach to the curriculum is likely to do just this, whereas arguably, what is needed is a pedagogy of enquiry that celebrates and utilises children's existing knowledge and understanding of the world, 'as they are already operating as young geographers and navigating the places and spaces in which they live' (Garner and Pickford, 2021, p. 195).

Poems can be a key aspect of this enquiry as they are a resource which might support the learning of particular subject matter or to make us look at the familiar through a different lens (Kirman, 2007). You might be exploring the water cycle with children (in science or geography), and this is an ideal topic to investigate through poetry as it has wonderful associated vocabulary – condense, evaporate, water droplets, precipitation, steam, vapour – which children might at first find difficult to grasp. Introducing this geographical language through poems can be a useful starting point and you can find some lovely examples, written by children, on the National Geographic Kids website – www.natgeokids.com/uk/discover/geography/physical-geography/raining-rhymes/. There is also a light-hearted example for younger children by Kristin Martin, called 'A Water Drop's Adventure', which you can find here – http://kristinmartin.net/?page_id=307.

Children usually have an authentic interest in the natural world and this interest can be used to good effect in geography lessons or topic work involved with an aspect of understanding the world in which we live. What is so powerful about using poems to capitalise on this interest is that they offer so many different viewpoints, depending on the background of the poet and the reason for their choice of subject matter. This raises an awareness that different viewpoints can lead to a better understanding of our world and the need to protect it in any way we can. There are some useful examples of nature poems here – www.palebluemarbles.com/nature-poems-for-kids-earth-day/ – short but powerful texts to promote discussions.

Although the natural world is a powerful and inspirational subject to inspire young geographers and poets, the man-made world also has much to offer and is an essential aspect of this curriculum area. Scoffham (2017, p. 26) explores the idea of using 'streetwork' as part of geographical enquiry, using the local area around a school to explore streets and buildings. He argues that this type of local learning outside the classroom promotes a valuing of children's surroundings and 'helps them develop a sense of belonging'. Learning outside the classroom is often perceived as needing considerable funding, time and attention to detailed risk assessments, with the idea of residential trips and activity centres being at the forefront of our minds. However, this need not be so and exploring the local area can have a significant impact on children's observation skills and bring about new perspectives of the familiar. The powerful thing about streetwork is that it is accessible to all children. They will all know the local streets and they will all have a home of some sort to live in. They will be familiar with windows and doors and roofs and bricks but are unlikely to have considered them in any depth before.

Scoffham (2017) includes a useful handout entitled 'Streetwork Features' with examples such as 'silhouette', 'focal point', 'texture' and 'repetition' – all aspects of the environment which give children the vocabulary to talk about what they see and describe features of their locality in detail, paying attention to the minutiae. All of this of course lends itself beautifully to poetry and there are many poems to be found that focus on houses, homes, towns, cities and buildings and children can write their own to capture the details of what they have observed in their locality. 'City Jungle' by Pie Corbett is a wonderful example to use with older children – https://jpsyearfour.weebly.com/uploads/2/0/4/4/20442177/english_-_performance_poetry.pdf – where the city is brought to menacing life through a series of powerful metaphors. Mandy Coe has put together a teaching resource which has three powerful poems which use the detail from observation to explore aspects of the environment www.mmu.ac.uk/media/mmuacuk/content/documents/mcbf/blog/MPL_Belonging_Street_Teaching_Resource.pdf. One of these is called 'The Tree That Saved the Town' and is a wonderful poem of hope. Children could think about how their own local area might be improved through simple and manageable projects. Activity 4 later in the chapter, provides an idea for how you might combine 'streetwork' and poetry.

Activities

Activity 1: Our histories

Narrative poems lend themselves beautifully to recording incidents in our lives – part of our histories. They do not need to rhyme, and the structure can be completely down to individual choice. Michael Rosen's 'Chocolate Cake' is a perfect example of this – www.youtube.com/watch?v=7BxQLITdOOc. When I used this poem with children, I would read/act it out, but I would not tell them it was a poem – I would just say, 'I'm going to read you something funny – I hope you enjoy it!' After the reading and some discussion, I would say, 'So, did you enjoy that poem?' and the children would usually look at me questioningly and ask why I had called it a poem when it is a story. I would then show them the poem written down, so that they could see the structure and we would have a useful discussion about narrative poems and the freedom you can have with this format.

With this activity, give the children time to discuss why they think Rosen wrote this poem. Is it from his own experience? Perhaps he has children of his own and this is part of their history. Children could then create a mind map, placing an incident from their own lives in the centre, and then all the aspects of this incident around the page, providing ideas and vocabulary for their poems. They may want to research other narrative poems to give them different ideas for style – some rhyming some non-rhyming. Emphasise that they are recording part of their history here and that it will be something lasting, enduring. It needs therefore to record as accurately and clearly as possible, so that others can picture the event and hold it in their minds.

A portfolio – either online or on paper – with the title 'Our Histories' could be made and shared with parents and other classes.

Activity 2: Poems from the archives

This activity relates to the earlier discussion in the chapter relating to 'found poetry', where children use primary historical sources to create poems, thus deepening their understanding of the historical event/person. For this activity you could focus on the era you are studying with your year group and ask them, first, to do some research, using original sources. On the National Archives site, you can search by historical period or by key stages or themes collections – there is so much there! With older children, they can do the research themselves, gathering ideas, words, phrases, images and anything that catches their attention from the sources, which tell the story of their chosen focus. With younger children, the research can be a shared activity, looking through the sources using the interactive whiteboard and gathering ideas together.

Spend plenty of time sharing what has been collected – perhaps do a table share where children leave their recorded ideas on their table and move around the room looking at the findings of their peers and having time to discuss. You then need to have a whole class debate, thinking about the different poetic forms that could be used in a 'Found Poem'. Examples of poems written with an historical theme can be shared at this point. There is a useful website – History for Kids – with poems for children about historical events, for example The Great fire of London – www.history-for-kids.com/great-fire-of-london.html. This has an animation to go with it and a child reading the poem. On this site you can search by era or topic and there is a good range of poems to choose from.

Either as a class or in small groups or individually, children then need to use the words and phrases they have collected to produce a poem, with an emphasis on a key aspect of the event or person being depicted. Explain to the children that they can focus in on a very small detail of their chosen event or person – they do not need to include everything. These poems could be recited in an assembly focusing on that period of history; they could be part of your history display; and they could certainly be shared with other classes, exploring the past through verse.

Activity 3: Getting the message out!

This activity brings together the subject of climate change and the environment, the use of persuasive language in radio advertisements and poetry writing skills.

Ask the children, 'What are advertisements trying to do?' List their ideas on the board; these might include:

- Persuade you to do something
- Persuade you to buy something
- Persuade you to think differently
- Persuade you to pass on the message to others

Listen to some advertisements from a local radio station and ask children to note down any persuasive devices. These might include songs, jingles, rhymes, tone of voice, word choice.

Often radio advertisements use specific devices to catch people's attention. Why do they need to do this? What is the difference between a radio advertisement and one on television or in a newspaper or magazine? Give children plenty of time to discuss so that they draw out the importance of presenting something that is aurally stimulating.

Provide time to look at some advertisements in newspapers and magazines, to watch some on television and then listen to some on a local radio station. Explain that the radio advertisements must last a certain amount of time and the advertiser has to pay so much per second – so they need to be short and catchy.

Ask the children to think about what aspect of their lives they would like to persuade the local community or the whole world to change, to support the environment and address issues of climate change. There is a very useful poem (suitable for younger children) which focuses on marine conservation and recycling, entitled 'Squiddly Diddly' – https://resources.poetrysociety.org.uk/wp-content/uploads/2021/07/NPD-2021-Resource-Poetry-Society.pdf – and there are also resources and ideas here. For older children, there are some wonderful poems here – www.theguardian.com/childrens-books-site/gallery/2015/apr/24/poems-of-our-earth-in-pictures – which celebrate the beauty of the earth but also present issues which need addressing.

Once the children have some ideas for content, they could then think about producing a catchy, very short poem which captures some of these ideas and persuades radio listeners to take action. This is a challenging activity and you will need to model and support. I have included an example below based on some of the ideas from Tony Bradman's poem, 'Leave the Whales Alone, Please!' which can be found at the website above.

Stop Hunting!
Stop hunting rare breeds
Leave them alive
We need them around
For us all to thrive.
(Virginia Bower)

Once the children have written their persuasive poems, they could be recorded and played to other classes or in an assembly. An accompanying display might be made, drawing on the artistic ideas presented on *The Guardian* website included above.

Activity 4: Streetwise, streetverse

Plan for a walk around the local area with your class and explain that the idea is to look at the familiar with fresh eyes; to notice details that we might normally walk by. As you walk the streets of your local community, draw attention to these details – the shapes made by roofs against the skyline, a view from a particular street corner that can only be seen from a certain angle; the colour of bricks and stonework and the texture of cement and railings. Children could record their observations, ideally into voice recorders rather than having to concern themselves with writing at this stage.

On return to the classroom, read the children James Berry's poem 'Childhood Tracks' – https://childrens.poetryarchive.org/poem/childhood-tracks/ – where Berry describes in detail his memories of childhood. Although this poem is not specifically about the streets where he lived, it is a great example of how, by recording what we have seen, smelled, heard and experienced, we can create a poem. Take some time to explore the poet's use of words, his use of repetition, the lack of rhyme and any other features that children notice.

Children choose one aspect of their own observations and build a poem around this. If you have already explored different poetic forms in previous lessons – haikus, rhyming couplets, free verse and so on – they can select the form that seems to best suit their ideas. If they do not have much experience of working with different forms, you could perhaps suggest one and model this, or they could use Berry's poem as a model.

These will be poems from their streets, from their communities and could be part of a project on local life. As a contrast, children could then use online sources to explore streets and towns in other areas of the globe and write poems to illustrate the differences they observe.

References

Alexander, R. (2009) 'Towards a Comparative Pedagogy', in Cowen, R. & Kasamias, A. M. (eds.) *International Handbook of Comparative Education*, New York, Springer, 911–929.
Andreotti, V. (2013) 'Taking Minds to Other Places', *Primary Geography*, Spring, 12–13.
BBC (2011) *Gove Stresses 'Facts' In School Curriculum Revamp*, Available at: www.bbc.com/news/education-12227491. Accessed on 30.01.2022.
Bower, V. (ed.) *Debates in Primary Education*, London: Routledge.
Department for Education (DfE) (2014) *National Curriculum*, London: DfE.
Department for Education (DfE) (2021) *Development Matters*, London: DfE.
Garner, W. & Pickford, T. (2021) 'Geography and History – A Sense of Time and Place', in Bower, V. (ed.) *Debates in Primary Education*, London: Routledge, 182–198.
Kirman, J. M. (2007) 'Aesthetics in Geography: Ideas for Teaching Geography Using Poetry', *Journal of Geography*, 106, 5, 207–214.
Lederle, C. (2012) *Making Connections Through Poetry: Finding the Heart in History*, Available at: https://blogs.loc.gov/teachers/2012/03/making-connections-through-poetry-finding-the-heart-in-history/. Accessed on 27.01.2022.
Lewis, P. (no date) *Teaching Content Subjects Using Poetry*, Available at: www.scholastic.com/teachers/articles/teaching-content/teaching-content-subjects-using-poetry/. Accessed on 27.01.2022.
Osbey, B. M. (2013) *The Poem as History*, Available at: www.warscapes.com/poetry/poem-history. Accessed on 27.01.2022.
Scoffham, S. (2017) 'Streetwork: Investigating Streets and Buildings in the Local Area', in Pickering, S. (ed.), *Teaching Outdoors Creatively*, London: Routledge, 26–41.
UNESCO (2014) *Roadmap for Implementing the Global Action Programme on Education for Sustainable Development*, Paris: UNESCO.

United Nations (2015) *Transforming Our World: The 2030 Agenda for Sustainable Development*, New York: UN Publishing.

Warwick, P. (2016) 'Education for Sustainable Development: A Movement Towards Pedagogies of Civic Compassion', *Forum*, 58, 3, 407-414.

Warwick, P., Warwick, A. & Nash, K. (2017) 'Towards a Pedagogy of Hope', in Huggins, V. & Evans, D. (eds.), *Early Childhood Education and Care for Sustainability: International Perspectives*, Abingdon: Routledge, 28-39.

8 Poetry in the digital age

One of the key aims of this chapter is to think about how we might use poetry to make the curriculum more accessible for children and how digital tools might support this. The chapter begins by examining how poetry 'fits' with digital learning and provides some examples of potential connections. The main section focuses on multimodality and how the modern, digital world allows children to innovate, experiment and explore, bringing their existing knowledge and understanding to classroom tasks, and transforming the learning experience. As with all the other chapters, there are practical suggestions for the classroom to finish.

Introduction

One of the questions we need constantly to ask ourselves is 'How relevant is the curriculum to our pupils growing up in the 21st century?' Regrettably, I suspect that for many children, the answer is – hardly at all relevant – and it is likely that children's existing literacy experiences go largely 'untapped' within the formal learning environment (Hughes, 2007, p. 3). In an ideal world, curriculum, pedagogy and assessment would be responsive to and in tune with children's experiences, to enable them to build a stable and navigable bridge between life in and out of school. Arguably, this is extremely challenging within a prescribed curriculum, where teacher agency is curtailed by, amongst other things, time and the pervasive threat of test results and accountability (Moon, 2002). However, it is rare for teachers to deliver a curriculum as it is presented and the curriculum is likely to undergo edits, additions, adaptations and even quite radical changes, to meet the needs of diverse contexts and learners (Alexander, 2009). This gives us hope for poetry and the use of poetry in digital contexts!

Children's experiences of and immersion in digital media might well result in a potential dissatisfaction with the transmission of knowledge through the 'delivery' of information by a human individual. They require education to be 'participative, engaging, and active' (Hazeldine, 2021, p. 207) and this is where the transformation of the curriculum comes in. This transformation draws on the existing knowledge and experience the children possess and, in a school context, they then become accustomed to finding information themselves, sifting and synthesising, retaining some elements and disregarding others; developing a critical approach to the often overwhelming quantity (and very variable quality) of material available online. This chapter suggests some ways that we might approach this and capitalise on what our young learners bring to our classrooms, bringing poetry into the digital age and enhancing the learning experience for all.

The chapter begins by examining how poetry 'fits' with digital learning and provides some examples of key links. The main section then focuses on multimodality and how the modern, digital world allows children to innovate, experiment and explore, bringing their existing knowledge and understanding to classroom tasks, and transforming the learning experience. As with all the other chapters, I finish with some practical suggestions for the classroom.

How does poetry 'fit' into digital learning?

When you think about 21st-century digital learning, poetry is probably not the first word that springs to mind! However, there are authentic synergies between the two and ways that they can work together to make children's classroom experience more meaningful, relevant and exciting. These include:

- the ability to engage learners on an individual level as well as providing ideal contexts for collaboration, communication and co-operation;
- the opportunity to be creative, to break the 'rules' and to bring yourself to the learning situation;
- the potential to work in multimodal ways to design and create outputs which reflect local and global interests and concerns.

I am going to explore the first two of these briefly, providing some examples in context, before moving on to the idea of multimodal approaches and examining the theory and practice behind these in more depth.

Individual and community engagement

For a variety of reasons, many of which have been outlined in other chapters, poetry is often perceived as the genre most difficult to access – for teachers and children. In their research, Hughes and Dymoke (2011, p. 49) found that trainee teachers' opinions of poetry included that it was boring, elitist, 'frill', difficult to evaluate and assess and a 'solitary art'. During the project, the trainees contributed their recommendations for poetry pedagogy which included starting with contemporary poetry (making it relevant), demystifying it, avoiding activities designed just to find the meaning in a poem, regular use of poetry and plenty of opportunities to collaborate. These findings indicate a real need to ensure poetry is relevant and accessible for all children and to ensure that individual learners have the freedom to work to their own agenda, but at the same time, raising their awareness of the power of collaboration and sharing ideas. Digital technology has the potential to achieve this, as individuals can use it in ways unique to them, but share, discuss, collaborate, evaluate and publish to the benefit of all.

As with all classroom practice, the effectiveness of bringing poems and technology together and allowing for both individual and collective engagement is dependent on the pedagogies employed and an innovative approach to the curriculum. In early years and primary, much of our time is spent gaining responses from children: their response to an image, a statement, a maths word problem, a scientific concept, a story or a poem. These are ideal times to bring individual ideas and collaboration together, so that children can share their personal thoughts and opinions whilst acknowledging that others may have a different response. You could start by presenting the children with a poem (or, depending on their age, they could research their own poems or make a choice from a selection you have offered) and asking them to begin by considering their personal response to this poem. If children are accustomed to this activity, they are then best to work on this alone before any further intervention. If not, you may need to model your responses to a particular poem.

Any examples you offer need to be open to interpretation, and haiku poems are ideal for this. The haiku originates in Japan and is often defined as a three-line poem with 17 syllables set in a 5-7-5 format. Although a consideration of this structure is useful if we are using poetic form as a scaffold (see Chapter 4 for detailed discussion of this), it is not something to insist on when encouraging children to explore and write their own haiku poems. Japanese syllables are of course not compatible with English syllables and indeed, it would be more appropriate – if the focus was to be on syllables – to utilise 12 English syllables. If we are using haiku within digital spaces, this is certainly *not* the main focus; instead, we want to encourage discussions, questions, debates and creative approaches to children's haiku reading, writing and presentation.

Take for example this haiku by Kobayashi Issa – a Japanese poet who wrote over 20,000 haiku poems in his lifetime:

> in leafy shade
> a melon for a pillow…
> a kitten
> 葉がくれの瓜を枕に子猫哉
> ha-gakure no uri wo makura ni ko neko kana

(You might wish to follow @issa_haiku on Twitter and you will be able to access a haiku every day. Not all of these will be suitable to use with children, but many are.)

Children could respond to this poem in any way they wish, but they need access to a device – laptop/iPad/PC – so that their response is in digital form. They could illustrate it with an image which they create digitally. They might respond with an oral (recorded) or typewritten anecdote about a pet of theirs and the strange places they choose to sleep, or they might just record themselves reciting the original poem (see Chapter 2 for a discussion relating to the importance of children finding their voice). They could write a poem in a similar style, describing a pet they have or that they have seen on the television or a video game or in a book. They might translate it into their own language (if they are EAL learners) or choose another language to create their own version, using Issa's haiku as a model (Google translate or DeepL are useful). Their responses need then to be added to a collaborative space – padlet is useful for this – which you will have created in advance, for every child to access. You can decide on the settings you think are appropriate so that children can perhaps 'like' other contributions or have the facility to give feedback. They could create a response to a fellow student's contribution, thereby growing a network of interrelated, personalised responses to a stimulus.

This is an example of what Hazeldine (2021) describes as the personalisation of learning in a digital environment. With this, individualised learning pathways are provided for children, where they can access, interact with and use multimodal texts in ways that suit them and which they can return to time and time again, strengthening and deepening their knowledge and understanding. With this type of activity, children can feel more in control of their learning, and they can retain a personal and individualised approach whilst communicating and collaborating to produce work that is better than what they might achieve alone. Hazeldine (2021, p. 203) describes this as 'an intensity of connection, interaction, exploration and discovery' – very different from 'chalk and talk' teacher-led lessons, with children as passive recipients of knowledge.

Breaking rules and bringing yourself to the learning experience

Poetry breaks the 'normal' rules of writing time and time again – what a joy! Wilson (2007, p. 453) argues that, with poems, children are required not only to 'unlearn rules' from other genres but also unlearn the rules of one poetic form against another (e.g., a sonnet and a kenning poem). He suggests that this can lead to a high cognitive load and needs to be approached with care and this is certainly a consideration and something to bear in mind when we introduce different poetic forms and structures. However, this rule-breaking can be turned into a powerful opportunity, particularly with the range of technology allowing us to be innovative with our approaches to design, structure and the use of multimodal elements.

An example of this might be introducing children to 'list' poems – poems where they do not need to worry about full stops, capital letters and other regular writing requirements. Instead, they can focus on the information they need to convey, the use of effective language and, for the sake of this chapter, how they will present their poems digitally. Figure 8.1 shows a very simple example of a list poem, focusing on a science topic – plants, trees and the environment. This has been produced using PowerPoint and then converting to a PDF for the purposes of this book. Depending on the technologies available, children can do much more – perhaps adding animations, sound, falling leaves and so forth. It is important to note, however, that there is a great deal to be achieved even with very basic computer programmes, and if we concern ourselves too much with the technology, it can become a barrier rather than a creative release.

In whatever way they decide to represent this scientific concept, the children are free to 'break the rules' of writing in that they are not handwriting or producing a linear piece of script and it may not bear any resemblance to what might be considered a 'normal' representation of a poem. They are not required to demonstrate their knowledge of this aspect of science in a traditional, predictable way and can put something of themselves into the presentation of the concept.

The example in Figure 8.1 is a list poem and also has some elements of 'concrete' or 'shape' poems. You can find another powerful example of a concrete poem, focusing on an aeroplane here: www.open.edu/openlearn/education/educational-technology-and-practice/educational-practice/word-and-image/content-section-2.3 and this poem is part of a free course from OpenLearn, entitled 'Word and Image' which you might be interested in investigating.

Figure 8.1 List poem

Children who often struggle with what might be described as the more 'traditional' approaches to literacy and learning, will undoubtedly revel in the freedom provided by 'rule-breaking' poems. You may find young learners whose output is usually limited and takes much coaxing to produce, are suddenly difficult to tear away from their work!

Multimodality and the digital age

Kress and van Leeuwen (no date), describe how we have moved from a 'monomodal' culture – separate disciplines such as art, music, linguistics – to a 'multimodal' society – within popular *and* high culture – where boundaries are blurred, and exciting opportunities emerge. Xerri (no date) provides a useful comparison between monomodal and multimodal approaches and I have summarised these in Figure 8.2.

Within a multimodal approach, it is 'quite possible for music to encode action, or images to encode emotion' (Kress and van Leeuwen, no date) and, with the technology we have available, we can potentially all try our hand at being authors, illustrators, music producers, orators. The emphasis is more on what choices to make that are most appropriate to the task or the decisions as to what effect we want to produce.

Life in the 21st century means that we are constantly adjusting to how meaning is conveyed in different ways using a range of formats and this links with how we often look for the meaning being conveyed by a poet in their unique ways. Poetry has the power to illuminate everyday objects or occurrences; to bring to our attention what is at first hidden and to put into words what is not easily expressed. There are clear links here with multimodal texts,

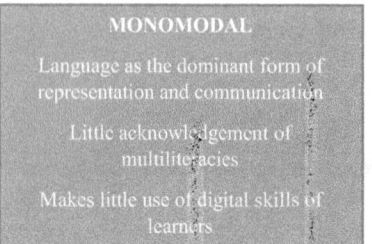

Figure 8.2 Monomodal and multimodal (adapted from Xerri [no date])

which often provoke us to think differently, see through different lenses and experience the familiar (and unfamiliar) in a range of ways. Hughes and Dymoke (2011, p. 55) suggest using multimodal ways 'to lift poetry from the printed page' and to reflect the reality of the lives of the children we teach.

At this point, although this chapter focuses on digital approaches, it is worthwhile considering Blake's (2015) argument that we do not necessarily require digital resources to engage with a multimodal approach to poetry and that the oral performance of a poem or the listening to a performance are manifestations of multimodal form. She writes that a reliance on technology often reflects a belief that poetry is a challenging genre and needs to be made more accessible – not perhaps the message we wish to convey. The main issue here is ensuring we understand *why* we are taking a particular approach and whether it is the best one for the learning we are seeking. And it is worth remembering that multimodality can take many forms. An authentically multimodal approach allows us to engage with our senses through the way that information is represented and communicated; described perfectly by Newfield and D'Abdon (2015, p. 515) when they refer to multimodality as, 'the making of meaning at different times and in different contexts, as well as the combination and orchestration of modes in multimodal ensembles at particular moments'.

In response to the plurality of possibilities in terms of multimodality in the classroom, I am going to look at three examples. The first focuses on spoken word poetry and how, in a digital age, we can exploit this by bringing performances into our classrooms from all over the world. The second is a more explicit use of a digital tool – Prezi – and how this allows for a multimodal approach to poetry. Finally, I will examine the idea of creating poetic movies.

Newfield and D'Abdon (2015) bemoan the fact that poetry curricula are barely changed since the 1980s and not relevant to children's lives. Often, there is little or no connection between the poetry children encounter and participate in outside school during social activities, family events, on the television, in advertising jingles and graffiti, song lyrics, rhymes and games and the poetry they encounter in school. To enable these connections to be made, two steps need to be taken: first, a commitment to a multimodal approach to poetry which recognises children's existing practices and experiences, and second, finding ways to change our own and others' perceptions of what 'counts' as poetry, giving it a 'different appearance' (ibid., p. 520). These two steps can be tackled through the use of spoken word poetry, focusing on poems from contemporary poets whose ideas are relevant and meaningful to learners. If you remember from Chapter 2, spoken word poetry is poetry written for oral performance, the multimodality of which is contained in the use of gesture, facial expressions, tone of voice, audience participation and so forth. Often, these oral performances have, as a theme, local and global events, opportunities and concerns and if we combine this with the possibilities that multimodality presents to empower children to find their own voices, it is a potent mix.

In a classroom context, it is likely that you would use audio- and audio-visual recordings of spoken word poetry to share with children, with the technology then available to replay, discuss, focus on particular aspects, and for children to re-engage with at times that suit them. There is a great example of spoken word poetry about favourite words and the power of words by Simon Mole to be found here – www.youtube.com/watch?v=UoudsbsU2ys.

Spoken word poetry does not need to be kept distinct from written poetry – quite the opposite in fact, as these two genres are inseparable. Written poems can be recited, enacted, recorded, replayed and so on, and oral poems can be written down, written about and act as models for a written version. However, the two approaches have aspects that are more suitable for certain writers and contexts and this is what needs examining and discussing with children. Some of them might prefer to be able to use gesture, intonation, facial expressions and audience interaction to get their message across. Others might prefer the affordances of written language and enjoy the way this looks on the page and how they can present their message. It certainly does not need to be one or the other – combinations are exciting and choice is essential as 'poetry must be able to speak a language that resonates with their everyday experiences, and be presented in a way that is meaningful to them' (Newfield and D'Abdon, 2015, p. 523).

Moving on now to looking at specific digital tools, and how they can be combined with poetry to create multimodal texts, I want to discuss the use of Prezi. The features of this software lend themselves beautifully to the presentation of poems in unique ways, which, in turn, allow for a deeper or different insight (Alghadeer, 2014). Prezi can be described as 'a virtual canvas and set of tools for preparing fluid and dynamic presentations using multimedia resources' (ibid., p. 91), whereby you receive an interconnected view of whatever is being presented and this can be in linear or non-linear form. Prezi has features such as the ability to zoom in and out, with the potential to highlight elements of a poem. Features such as these encourage participatory and active learning, experimentation, innovation and individual responses. Susanti et al. (2019) worked with primary aged children, examining the impact of using Prezi on their writing of poetry. They found that this design tool encouraged participatory and active learning, experimentation, innovation and individual responses. Aspects of students' writing improved, particularly their use of vocabulary, as did their attitudes to writing, and they were more actively involved with the learning.

If we think back to Chapter 1, where I used the example of Auden's 'Night Mail', with the train rumbling along the tracks, you can start to think about how powerful it would be to use Prezi to bring this poem to life. Prezi allows for the embedding of videos, and the YouTube version of Night Mail could be included alongside the presenting of the stanzas, appearing on the screen as the film progresses. Designing this presentation would necessitate a thorough engagement with the vocabulary, the wonderful imagery, the rhythms and cadences and how these change through the poem. Children would need to think about why the poet has created this effect and decide how best to reproduce this in their presentation. The learning potential of a Prezi poetry project throws into shade the oft-mundane learning objectives we see diligently copied down by jaded pupils into their one-dimensional, linear workbooks. Surely, we owe them more than this?

Bayley (2016, p. 392) metaphorically and beautifully describes poems as 'a portable cinema screen with a film that helps us to confront the enigmatic, shifting, seductive, potentially traumatic and insistent world around us'. Making the metaphorical real is the intention of the final example of a multimodal approach in this section, with the use of film-making software to represent poems. Templer (2009, p. 2) refers to these as 'visualised poems' or 'poetry in motion', and argues that the power of these multimodal texts lies in the combination of sound, vision and language and that many of us are more likely to remember concepts if words and images are combined. Ghazali (2008) found that more than 80 per cent of participants in her study – focusing on students' perceptions of accessing literary texts – expressed a preference for the use of audio-visual materials to support understanding. Templer provides a lovely example of a visualised poem which would be interesting to share with children, entitled 'Walking Across the Atlantic' – www.youtube.com/watch?v=oaF-qU5aMuk. Once children have seen some examples of these 'visualised poems' you can guarantee they will be keen to try for themselves!

Alghadeer (2014) suggests using Movie Maker, to 'remake' poems and this approach has so much potential in terms of enhancing children's learning experience. Through creating a 'poetic movie' the children gain a better understanding of the poem. They can interpret poems in ways that work for them and be innovative with how they choose to represent these interpretations, thus inspiring 'new possibilities for active meaning making within a multitude of digital explorations and applications' (ibid., p. 93). Alghadeer refers to how the short films children make can build connections between the work of art (the poem), the poet and the audience. If the chosen poems are related to local, national or international themes, these would be extremely powerful creations and have the potential to spread important societal messages through the school community. In Activity 2, towards the end of the chapter, I provide a more specific example that you might want to use in the classroom.

Taking a multimodal approach to poetry pedagogy – with or without digital tools – has the potential to transform our learning spaces. Here are some of the reasons:

- Learners are empowered by the diverse approaches and how they can choose a mode/modes to suit their preferences. This gives them more of a voice and an opportunity to actively engage and take responsibility for their learning;
- Language is provided in a variety of ways – orally, written, gesture, sign – and is therefore more inclusive, particularly for EAL learners and those with special educational needs;
- A multimodal approach provides the relevance with children's lives in terms of the 'multiliteracies' (Newfield and D'Abdon, 2015, p. 528) encountered in everyday life;
- A multimodal approach has the potential to 'turn classrooms into dynamic, up-to-date learning environments, liberating poetry from textbooks and awakening students' dormant appetite for language play and multisemiotic representation' (ibid.).

At first this approach to poetry might seem somewhat daunting, particularly if we also find the array of technologies at our disposal quite bewildering. However, do not be apprehensive! The ideas discussed above, and the activities described below will almost always result

Poetry in the digital age 105

in being led by the children; and that is exactly what we want. Use their existing knowledge of digital tools, give them freedom to explore, and use the time effectively to support, assess and enjoy the many different aspects of learning that will undoubtedly be taking place.

Activities

These activities have emerged from the section in Alghadeer's (2014) article, referred to earlier in the chapter, where the author discusses remaking poetic texts using 'digital modalities'. Seven examples are given by Alghadeer: Twitter and haiku; Instagram and photograph poems; Prezi and virtual poetics; Poetry movie maker; Poetry blogs; Digital collage poetry; and Poetry posters. Some of these have been mentioned earlier in the chapter and the activities below will provide practical examples building on more of these digital modalities.

Activity 1: Instagram and photograph poems

The idea here is that children have the chance to use photographs which they feel align most effectively with a chosen poem, whereby 'several meanings, intricate sorts of emotions, and overwhelming experiences can emerge' (ibid., p. 91). The act of finding a poem that they want to represent – a poem that, for some reason 'speaks' to them – selecting photographs from a personal bank or from photographs offered by family and friends and then deciding how to use them – allows them to create their own interpretation of the poem and develop a range of skills.

When thinking about an example I might use to show older children, I decided I would use the poem by Tupac Shakur entitled, 'The Rose That Grew from Concrete' – https://allpoetry.com/The-Rose-That-Grew-From-Concrete. My interpretation of this poem is that whatever your background, you can make something of yourself and flourish in life. The photographs I would therefore share with the children might be of my school reports (particularly damning!!), and my first degree, masters and doctoral certificates – showing my own education journey – from an inauspicious start in secondary age schooling to a PhD – a personal interpretation of the rose growing from concrete (although visualising myself as the rose might be a step too far!).

When conducting this activity with children, time needs to be taken for them to access and enjoy a wide range of poems. With young children, you could read them two or three poems each day for a couple of weeks, before starting the main task. Children could give each poem a star rating, so that when they come to decide on a poem to use, they have their favourites to re-read. Next, decisions need to be made about photographs to use. These could be existing photos or children may need to take their own to fit how they wish to illustrate the key ideas of the poem they have chosen. A simple example might be to use a poem mentioned in Chapter 4 – Eleanor Farjeon's poem 'Cats Sleep Anywhere' – www.scrapbook.com/poems/doc/8991.html – particularly useful if children in your class have cats! This poem is straightforward, and children could create a wonderful montage of photos, showing their pets in different areas of the house. These could be part of a slideshow, with the poem being read in the background.

A more challenging poem for older children might be 'Inside a Shell' by John Foster - https://childrens.poetryarchive.org/poem/inside-a-shell/. This is such a beautiful poem, with lots to discuss and debate, and is a powerful model for children to use as a starting point for their own poetry writing (see Chapter 4 for more discussion on the use of models). But for this activity, it provides useful images for which children might find photographs and then choose to bring the poem and their photos together in a way that works for them.

Activity 2: Poetry blogging and vlogging

Blogs and vlogs are useful ways to bring together independent and collaborative learning, as discussed earlier in the chapter, to enable children to engage in different ways to suit their preferences. A class/school blog/vlog site could be set up so that children can share their opinions about poems they have read or listened to. They could upload favourites, record recitals and add these, and include recommendations and links. There is an example of a blog - *Poetry for Children* - here - http://poetryforchildren.blogspot.com/ - and this might give you some ideas about how you could set up a similar style blog spot for children. This could be for all ages, as, with younger children, you could use the blog as a class and upload their ideas and choices during carpet time, or parents could be encouraged to work with children on this.

Activity 3: Multimodal haiku

Alghadeer (2014) suggests using Twitter as a platform for multimodal haiku, but in early years and primary schools, it might be more useful to think about how children can record the poems they produce in ways that can be shared easily across the school community. This might be through a television screen in the entrance hall showing a rolling programme of contributions or on the school website. It could be within the blog/vlog as described in the previous activity.

With this activity, the children might choose an existing haiku or create one of their own. The idea then is to represent it using three images - one for each line. These could be photographs, drawings, cartoons, videoed actions, marks in a sandpit and so on. Through this representation, children need to think carefully about the meaning behind the words they - or the poet - have used. Figure 8.3 shows an example of a haiku I have written and then how I chose to represent my ideas. I am certainly not a talented poet, although I enjoy the process of writing poems, so do not be put off by thinking that you cannot write poems yourself. Children will enjoy any examples you share and are very good critics who can help you improve! Be brave and put yourself out there!

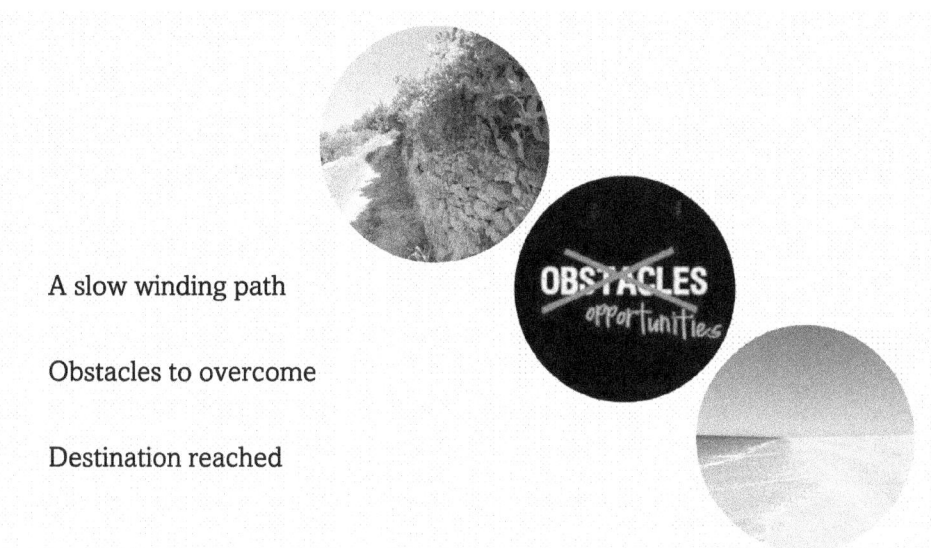

A slow winding path

Obstacles to overcome

Destination reached

Figure 8.3 Haiku poem

References

Alexander, R. (2009) 'Towards a Comparative Pedagogy', in Cowen, R. & Kasamias, A. M. (eds.), *International Handbook of Comparative Education*, New York: Springer, 911–929.

Alghadeer, H. A. (2014) 'Digital Landscapes: Rethinking Poetry Interpretation in Multimodal Texts', *Journal of Arts and Humanities*, 2, 87–96.

Bayley, N. (2016) '"A Long-Legged Fly Upon the Stream": Poetry, Memory and the Unconscious', *Changing English*, 23, 4, 387–395.

Blake, J. (2015) 'Poetry, Listening and Learning', in Dymoke, S., Barrs, M., Lambirth, A. & Wilson, A. (eds.), *Making Poetry Happen Transforming the Poetry Classroom*, London: Bloomsbury, 107–113.

Ghazali, S. N. (2008) 'Learners' Background and Their Attitudes Towards Studying Literature', *Malaysia Journal of ELT Research MELTA*, 4, 1–17.

Hazeldine, L. (2021) 'Using Digital Strategies for Primary Learning', in Bower, V. (ed.), *Debates in Primary Education*, Abingdon: Routledge, 199–217.

Hughes, J. (2007) *Poetry: A Powerful Medium for Literacy and Technology Development*, What Works? Research into Practice, Ontario: The Literacy and Numeracy Secretariat.

Hughes, J. & Dymoke, S. (2011) '"Wiki-Ed Poetry": Transforming Preservice Teachers' Preconceptions About Poetry and Poetry Teaching', *Journal of Adolescent & Adult Literacy*, 55, 1, 46–56.

Kress, G. & van Leeuwen, T. (no date) 'Kress and van Leeuwen on Multimodality', Available at: https://newlearningonline.com/literacies/chapter-8/kress-and-van-leeuwen-on-multimodality. Accessed on 16/12/2021.

Moon, B. (2002) 'Understanding the Context of Curriculum', in Moon, B., Shelton-Mayes, A. & Hutchinson, S. (eds.), *Teaching, Learning and the Curriculum in the Secondary School*, London: RoutledgeFalmer, 191–193.

Newfield, D. & D'Abdon, R. (2015) 'Reconceptualising Poetry as a Multimodal Genre', *TESOL Quarterly*, 49, 3, 510–532.

Susanti, A., Mustadi, A., Asnimar, A. & Susiloningsih, E. (2019) 'The Improvement in Poetry Writing Skills by Using Prezi in the Primary School', *Mimbar Sekolah Dasar*, 6, 1, 92–104.

Templer, B. (2009) *Poetry in Motion: A Multimodal Teaching Tool*. Available at: www.researchgate.net/publication/26852043_Poetry_in_Motion_A_Multimodal_Teaching_Tool. Accessed on 04.01.2022.

Wilson, A. (2007) 'Finding a Voice? Do Literary Forms Work Creatively in Teaching Poetry Writing?', *Cambridge Journal of Education*, 37, 3, 441-457.

Xerri, D. (no date) *The Multimodal Approach to Using Poetry in ELT*, Available at: www.danielxerri.com/uploads/4/5/3/0/4530212/multimodal_approach_to_using_poetry_in_elt_xerri.pdf. Accessed on 05.01.2022.

9 Getting creative with poetry

In this chapter, there is a focus on the arts – more specifically painting, song, dance and drama – and how poetry might be used (as an art form in its own right) in conjunction with these, to enhance children's experience. The chapter includes a practical classroom activity for each of these art forms, with examples of how poems can be used in a range of ways.

Introduction

Although this whole book is fundamentally about 'getting creative', and reference to art forms other than poetry occur through most chapters, I nevertheless felt it was essential to include a chapter specific to the arts. Any opportunity to shine a spotlight on the arts needs embracing wholeheartedly and coupling poetry with its fellow art disciplines is one way to try for more curriculum coverage that gives the arts the attention they deserve and our children the broad and balanced curriculum they merit.

Ruck Keene (2020, p. 109) explores the idea of the instrumental and the intrinsic benefits of the arts, highlighting 'the fundamental disconnect present in the promotion of the economic value of the arts without promoting the intrinsic educational value of artforms, and associated skill development'. Despite championing the intrinsic value of the arts, Ruck Keene concludes that a focus on the usefulness of these subjects is more likely to result in raised attention, funding and status – much needed in current times. For many reasons, an insistent focus on 'core' subjects and the consequent narrowing of the curriculum, lack of funding, the arts seen as 'soft' subjects, lack of support for the arts from our political leaders (Paton, 2014) – to name but a few – the arts within the curriculum have become a luxury rather than a given. It comes down to us as teachers taking agency, recognising the myriad affordances of the arts and promoting them at every opportunity. Ruck Keene concludes her chapter saying:

> Ultimately, for the arts to have a viable future within primary schooling systems, individual educators and leaders of education must form their own perspectives on why they matter; the fundamental issue is to realise that they do.
>
> (2020, p. 119)

The arts can include of course painting, sculpture, mosaics, theatre, dance, music, architecture and so forth (Britannica, no date), and I have needed therefore to be selective within this chapter, choosing to focus on painting, music (focusing on song), dance and drama (as these are more likely to be on the agenda in early years and primary settings), and how we can explore these areas through poetry. However, hopefully many of the ideas will resonate, whichever of the arts you are enjoying with your pupils.

Poetry and painting

Leonardo da Vinci famously said: 'Painting is poetry that is seen rather than felt, and poetry is painting that is felt rather than seen' which articulates the link between the two whilst leaving room for debate and disagreement – do we not see and feel paintings? Do we not feel and see poems? With older children, it could be interesting to present them with this quote and ask for their thoughts. More important though is to think about how you can connect these art forms in early years and primary classrooms, to promote a deeper appreciation of both. Kleppe (2018) believes that painting and poetry, taught together (known as ekphrasis), can enhance the learning experience for all ages, from very young infants to the elderly. This might include a simple activity such as examining and discussing illustrations of poems – in nursery rhyme books for example – or more complex arts-based responses (Jusslin and Höglund, 2021, p. 39) – 'using art forms to respond to a literary or written text' – allowing children freedom to record their reaction to a poem through artwork.

On the J. Paul Getty Museum website – www.getty.edu/education/teachers/classroom_resources/curricula/poetry_and_art/ – you will find connections between poetry and art emphasised, with a focus on how, over the centuries, 'art has inspired poets and poetry has inspired artists'. On this site, you can find lesson ideas and activities for all age children and useful videos which provide ideas on how to bring poetry and art together. You might also be interested in the Van Gogh House London website – https://vangoghhouse.co.uk/learning/vincents-treasures/poetry-and-painting/ – where there are some wonderful ideas for the classroom, based on approaches taken by Van Gogh whose artwork was often inspired by poetry. You could adapt some of these activities for the age children you teach or, if you work with older children, let them explore this site and work through the activities themselves – there is a great deal here they can enjoy. In the same way that artwork can be inspired by poetry, so poetry can be inspired by artwork. On the arts desk website – https://theartsdesk.com/visual-arts/listed-poems-inspired-paintings – there are examples of ten poems that took their inspiration from paintings. The paintings and the poems are included and, with some adapting for different age children, these could be a very powerful resource.

Art appreciation can be challenging for young children and they may not have the vocabulary to express how they feel. This is just one way in which poetry can be a powerful resource. In 2013 in the MoMa galleries in New York an experiment was trialled, in an attempt to address the difficulties encountered by some visitors when trying to appreciate the works of art amidst crowds and without support with interpreting what was displayed (Armstrong, 2013). Artists and poets were invited to conduct readings, standing in front of different works of art and then visitors were invited to respond to a survey to indicate how they found this experience. Evidence suggested that the 'combination of poetry and visual art breathed life into the respective mediums and transformed the galleries into a place of active looking and listening' (ibid.). Visitors reported that, whilst the reading was taking place, it gave them time to take in the artwork, spend time just looking and for some, it made them look at pieces of art from new perspectives. Nearly 100 per cent of the respondents reported that their gallery visit was enhanced and that they felt more involved in the experience. Armstrong finishes her blog with these words:

> It's incredible how much an experience is enriched when art forms are combined, one illuminating the other and requiring the use of multiple senses. Not only do poetry readings layer words over the experience of looking at painting, they also add the element of performance. It is this combination that seems to transform observers into participants and prompt them to notice things they might otherwise have missed.

In her article, 'Why we should treat poetry like painting', Besner (2012) has some innovative ideas which would be great fun to enact in the classroom. Besner writes that she is envious of the art gallery environment and proposes that, if *poetry* galleries were introduced, where people could wander in calm, well-lit spaces with 'curatorial text to explain things about the poems that might not be obvious', then poetry would be more accessible and enjoyable for all. Usually, in art galleries, exhibits are accompanied by some background information and maybe even an audio commentary. This could work well for poems, which might 'gain aesthetically if they were freed from the burden of explanation'. Besner admits that poets often feel that their poems should speak for themselves; but this is not of course always the case for most of us and some support would be much appreciated – to promote appreciation!

Besner goes on to describe her ideal poetry gallery and I reproduce it in full here, as I think it can provide an inspiration for our own classrooms and wider school environments:

> I would love it if all major cities had a poetry museum, where you could go for a visit dressed up in your best all-black clothes. The poems would be widely spaced on clean white walls, big enough for four or five people at once to stand in front of them and read. You could go there on dates for the free Tuesday nights, and you could take your parents there when they came to visit. There would be architecturally remarkable staircases and third-floor cafés where you could eat arugula salads. You could wander from poem to poem, pressing buttons on your headset to hear a curator with a British accent talk about the poet's life and the political situation where they live and the echoes of other poets' work in the poem you're looking at. There would be rooms representing various strands of poetic practice, and when you travelled to other countries and visited their poetry museums, you could learn about their major poets, past and present, in one pleasant afternoon. You could buy books and posters in the gift shops.

Think about how you might adapt this idea. Children's poems – either those they write themselves or examples from their favourite poets – could be enlarged as part of a display, perhaps with paintings alongside. Each poem could have a commentary, researched and written by the children, giving background and interesting facts. If you have mini voice recorders, these could be attached to the display with audio commentaries. Other classes and parents could be invited to your poetry and painting gallery, perhaps attending in their 'gallery clothes' and drinks and nibbles could be provided. What a memorable experience this would be!

Poetry and song

Poetry and songs have always been very closely linked; indeed 'the first lyric poets in ancient Greece performed their work to the accompaniment of the lyre, and the oldest anthology of Chinese poetry, the Shijing, was a collection of songs' (Poetry Foundation, no date) and it is only over time that they have evolved as separate artforms. Arguably, this separation occurred as a result of the advent of writing and printing, leading to poems being read rather than recited and listened to – it was in the reciting that the musicality emerged.

With the passing of time, debates have arisen around the different opinions about the links between songs and poems, songwriters and poets. There is much debate as to whether song lyrics can be regarded as poems and whether songwriters should be accorded the same 'status' as poets. Arguably, this has a great deal to do with who Wheeler (2016) describes as the 'cultural gatekeepers' – those who wish to decide what is high and low culture and what should 'fit' into which cultural category. This is significant for the children we teach, as they have a right to form their own views and a right to access a wide range of poetry, music and all other art forms. It has to be remembered that not all children will have this access outside school and therefore whatever we can do to expose them to a wide variety and also to introduce them to the accompanying debates, provides them with the cultural capital needed in our fast-paced world.

The debate around songs and poems, songwriters and poets came to a head when, in 2016, the Nobel Prize committee awarded the literature prize to Dylan 'for having created new poetic expressions within the great American song tradition', with the Permanent Secretary of the Swedish Academy insisting that Dylan 'can be read and should be read, and is a great poet in the grand English poetic tradition' (cited in Webb, 2017). Interestingly, the prize-winner himself said, 'songs are unlike literature. They're meant to be sung, not read'.

One of the key questions is whether a song is simply a poem put to music and, of course, the actuality is far more complex as some songs are extremely poetic and many poems have a song-like quality.

Webb (2017) writes that 'Poems, generally speaking, behave on the page, and operate against silence. Song lyrics, generally speaking, perform in sound, and operate in a relationship with musical apparatus'. There are arguments to be made against these claims also and these would be useful debating points in the classroom. It is good for children to realise that there are no concrete, 'right' answers and that having an opinion and being able to defend and justify is what matters. Indeed, Webb goes on to question,

> Does any of this matter – need the boundaries between song and poem be patrolled and policed? Possibly not. After all, as 18th-century Italian philosopher Giambattista Vico suggests, we humans came to language through song; and song and poetry together built the linguistic domain we now inhabit.

However, she does acknowledge that categorisation can have significant, pragmatic outcomes, for example popular musicians can earn considerable sums of money; a rarity for poets.

In an interview on the United States National Public Radio Station (NPR) in 2006, Leonard Cohen discussed the difference between poems and songs and his words really help us to think about the differences.

> Well, there are certain – there are certain poems that really do lie very gracefully on the page. For instance, to take an obvious example, if – a poem by E.E. Cummings has a certain graceful display on the page. And some poems just naturally are meant to be absorbed in silence, where the tempo is decided on by the reader. And he could reverse it and forward it and linger.
>
> There are other kinds of lyrics that have their own metrical, imperial advice. And they invite you to move swiftly from line to line. And there are poems that are – of mine – that are always candidates for a song. Sometimes they don't make it and sometimes they do.

This quote could be the basis for a powerful classroom investigation. Children could explore poems of their own choice and work in groups to discuss and decide whether particular poems are 'candidates for a song' and, more importantly, why. They could compose their own melody to suit a particular poem. They might also want to decide which poems demonstrate Cohen's 'graceful display on the page' and therefore are best suited to remain as poems. These activities develop a critical approach to poems and songs, whilst at the same time giving children opportunities to have fun, explore and make their own decisions.

Many years ago, I introduced writing journals to my Year 6 class, basing my ideas on Graham and Johnson's United Kingdom Literacy Association minibook – *Children's Writing Journals* (2012). Each child was given a blank journal and they could write whatever and whenever they wished in these booklets. They could choose whether to share their writing with their friends or with me. There was much that emerged from this project, but one of the most interesting outcomes was the way that most children became absorbed in writing song lyrics. Once one child started, it spread like a friendly contagion and made me realise how little I engaged with the popular culture that most interested them. Any introduction of activities relating to songs and lyrics will, I suspect, be embraced wholeheartedly by your class!

Poetry and dance

There are many connections between poetry and dance which can be exploited with early years and primary age children to ensure enjoyment of both and provide memorable learning experiences. So what are these links? Anderson (2010, p. 252) writes that poetry and dance are both 'arts of motion through space and time' and although dance involves actual physical body movement, poetry is both spatial and temporal because of how the words appear on the page or how they are read – the rhythms, inflections and tones. Anderson refers to this as 'verbal choreographic patterning' and this patterning will determine how a poem is read (either internally or aloud) in the same way that the patterns of dance will speak in different ways to an audience.

Poems and dance moves can 'suggest manifold implications through simple means' (ibid., p. 258), although of course they are rarely as simple as they might first appear and the planning that goes into the final product is detailed and complex, with consideration of the choice of movements or words; the order they are presented; the impact this is likely to have on an audience/reader. Anderson highlights the unpredictable nature of both poetry and dance and the way that they have the capacity to surprise – a major reason perhaps why they entertain and delight us.

Babcock (2016, p. 128) undertook a five-year project which brought together collaborative pedagogies, dance and haiku poems. She shared haiku poems with her students and asked them to consider whether they were able to 'find or connect to possibilities for shapes, for actions, for stillness' within the poems. Because a haiku is all about finding the essence of something and representing this, the students could then work on finding the essence of a movement for their dances. The findings showed several positive outcomes including positive interactions and effective collaboration, emotional connectedness, a better understanding of space and timing in dance choreography, the development of a closer-knit class community, active participation, levelling of hierarchy – the teacher becoming the learner – inclusive practice, negotiating skills and conflict resolution, and clear utilisation of existing knowledge and experience.

Babcock (2016, p.127) concluded that 'Merging dance with poetry through collaborative learning provides a deeper, richer understanding of the process' and for the researcher, this process was more focused on dance. However, the understanding can of course work both ways with a poem encouraging deeper thinking about how to represent the meaning through dance moves; and the dance moves revealing levels of meaning with a poem. Here is an example to illustrate this, using the poem 'The Seagulls' by Michael Rosen – https://childrens.poetryarchive.org/poem/the-seagulls/. Play the audio version of the poet reading the poem. Give children a written version and, working in groups, ask them to draw out key vocabulary that might be represented by dance moves, for example 'swoop', 'sea-breezes', 'screaming', 'hover'. How might these moves be repeated, joined together and performed? Opportunity then needs to be given for children to practise their dance moves in a large space, putting together a sequence. These can then be performed against the backdrop of Michael Rosen reading the poem.

Activity 3 towards the end of the chapter has a further example you might want to explore with your class.

Poetry and drama

In Chapter 2, I explored aspects of performance poetry and how this can be a useful pedagogy to support the development of both speaking and listening skills and this section builds on those ideas. For performing, poems are ideal as, unlike stories or plays, they do not need to have a cast of characters and there can be a single voice which the performer can inhabit. Also, many poems are of manageable length, making them accessible for all and providing the opportunity, over a relatively short period of time, for exposure to a great many examples.

In Athanases' (2005, p. 88) project, pupils were supported with choosing, reading, rehearsing and performing poems. He describes the way that the pupils 'lived with' a poem for a whole week, with repeated readings, rehearsals, written reflections and performances. Athanases found that the repeating of a poem through many rehearsals, followed by written reflections, led the students through a time of discovery where they came to a deeper understanding of how to make meaning from what they read, and how interpretations and therefore performances can differ. Rehearsing and performing takes you from being an outsider, reading the poem and peering into it from the periphery to being inside the poem, living and breathing it as the character. One of the students described it as needing 'more of a commitment' to the poem; not so much studying a poem but engaging with it.

One of the drama techniques used by Athanases in his study was to ask the pupils to repeat lines of poems in different ways – sadly, angrily, questioningly, laughingly. In this way, they began to consider the sub-text of the poem and were able to perform in ways that portrayed 'particular embodied feelings and meanings' (ibid., p. 89). This is a powerful pedagogy to employ and requires children to go beyond a surface reading of a text. However, it can be great fun and enjoyed by children of all ages. You could use a poem such as 'Best Friends' by Bernard Young – https://bernardyoung.co.uk/poems/. This is a powerful poem which is likely to resonate with children's experiences. You could read the poem in a fairly neutral way, allowing the children to absorb the surface meaning. Then, ask a volunteer to read the first two stanzas in an angry, loud voice. How does this change the impact of the poem? Ask another volunteer to read the same two stanzas in a sad voice. What difference does this make? Set the children off in groups to explore the final stanzas and decide how they might perform these, as there is a significant shift in the poem at this point. Give plenty of time for rehearsal and discussion followed by performances. One way to set up the performances is to ask each group how they would like stanza one and two to be read – with what tone and at what volume? You could then perform these and they follow on with their interpretation of the final stanzas. Children will enjoy seeing the ways others have construed the poem and they will benefit from performances which demonstrate different perspectives of the same poem.

For younger children, there is a poem entitled, 'Celebrating Six' by Kelly Roper – https://parenting.firstcry.com/articles/15-best-birthday-poems-for-kids/. This poem has three very short stanzas and could be performed in a whispered, hushed voice or in an excited tone or perhaps in a wondering way. Young children can be encouraged to reflect on how this seems to change the meaning behind the words. Although support might be needed with this, to give the children the vocabulary needed for voicing their ideas, I do not believe that children are ever too young to engage with this kind of activity and so much is to be gained.

We want children to arrive at a better understanding of poems without going through the dry process of over-analysis which is unfortunately the experience of many learners. Drama has the capacity to allow for this and can motivate pupils because of its multimodal, multisensory nature. Ferguson (2014, p. 1) writes that 'to perform a poem, a student must use critical thinking and comprehension skills such as activating prior knowledge, questioning, visualizing, inferencing, summarizing and synthesizing to explore both the literal and the unsaid within a poem'. These are comprehension skills that we are all looking to promote with our young learners and, using drama and poems, takes us a very long way from the 'read a passage and answer the questions' worksheets tasks, so often imagined when we mention reading comprehension.

Ferguson (2014) suggests a variety of dramatic techniques to explore poetry including choral reading, readers' theatre, soundscapes and tableaux (freezeframes). Choral reading and performing can occur in different ways – the whole class performing together, groups reading particular lines or stanzas – and these all require repeated readings, a discussion of content to decipher the meaning and therefore how the poem should be performed, and an evaluation of the choral performance. These are all powerful skills which allow pupils to approach poems with more tools at their disposal and help to prevent an initial response to a new poem of 'I don't understand this'. Instead, they will have strategies to allow them to explore beneath the surface of the words.

Readers' theatre is a useful way to engage with poems which have dialogue. As a class, you could work towards producing a playscript from the poem. Parts can be assigned and the play enacted. Others could produce a choral reading of the poem and the two representations could then be compared.

Soundscapes are like landscapes – they provide a powerful backdrop. Using body percussion or actual musical instruments, children can decide which sounds best represent lines of a poem. A volunteer can then read the poem slowly, with the accompanying chosen sounds for each line. This can be repeated but without the reading of the poem – just the sounds. All of these activities require children to think more deeply about words used and the meaning the poet is conveying; but they are not the dry, formulaic approaches whereby children are asked, 'What do you think the poet is saying here?' which can be very daunting to any learner. Instead, through active engagement, children are probing beneath the surface and drawing out meaning.

Activity 4 below explores freezeframes – sometimes known as tableaux – and these are powerful ways to develop comprehension of poems and also to allow for ongoing formative assessment, as you as the teacher have the chance to step back and observe. Essentially, this drama technique requires children to represent an idea through a still pose. You could set each group a line or a stanza or they could create a freezeframe to represent the whole poem – it would be interesting here to see the different interpretations of each group.

Activities

I have included an activity for each of the four areas explored in the chapter – painting, song, dance and drama.

Activity 1: A colourful world

Rainbows are magical and make for wonderful subject matter to explore through poetry and art (not to mention the links you could make with geography – weather and seasons – and science). Start by asking the children: Who has seen a rainbow before? Who knows the colours of the rainbow? Does anyone know how you can remember these colours? The children may well know some sayings or songs to help them remember. If not, you could give them some examples, for example 'Richard of York gave battle in vain'.

Read Walter de la Mare's poem, 'The Rainbow':

> I saw the lovely arch
> Of Rainbow span the sky,

> The gold sun burning
> As the rain swept by.
>
> In bright-ringed solitude
> The showery foliage shone
> One lovely moment,
> And the Bow was gone.

You could also read Christina Rossetti's poem with the same title:

> Boats sail on the rivers,
> And ships sail on the seas;
> But clouds that sail across the sky
> Are prettier far than these.
>
> There are bridges on the rivers,
> As pretty as you please;
> But the bow that bridges heaven,
> And overtops the trees,
> And builds a road from earth to sky,
> Is prettier far than these.

Discuss the different colours of a rainbow and access some images of rainbows online, so that the children have a clear idea of the different colours in their heads. Give each group a colour and ask them to create a mind map with the colour in the middle and then any words, phrases and ideas linked with that colour around the outside. You may want to model using the more difficult colours – indigo and violet. You should end up with seven mind maps with plenty of ideas about colours to help the children when they write their poems and these could be photocopied so that each group has access to all seven versions.

The children now need time to discuss colour mixing and to consider the style of rainbow they wish to paint. There are some lovely examples of different styles at the Tate Kids site – www.tate.org.uk/kids/explore/top-5/top-5-rainbows. They can then begin creating their rainbows on a size of paper to suit them, using wide bands of colour (space is needed to insert their lines of poetry onto each band). They might prefer to explore collage techniques, using different materials (potential link with science here).

Leave the artwork to dry while the children create their own rainbow poems, using the words collected earlier (with younger children, you may want to create one poem altogether). Explain that they need one line for each colour, as they are going to transfer each line along the arch of each colour of the rainbow. When the paintings/collages are dry, children can decide how they intend to transpose their poems onto their rainbows and they will need to think creatively here. Let them consider how to solve this challenge – resist the temptation to step in with your own ideas!

These rainbow poems will make an incredible display. If you do not have time for children to all create their own, you could create one very large rainbow, with each group working on a coloured arch, which could span a wall space, and have a shared writing session to produce a class poem to transfer to the artwork.

Activity 2: Let's get lyrical!

If you read song lyrics as if they are a poem, they often sound very different from when they are sung and if you sing a poem as if it is a song, it has the potential to lift the words from the page and make them more than the original. Earlier in the chapter I discussed the debates around songs and poems and whether song lyrics are poetry. The debate is an interesting one, but whatever your thoughts on this, song lyrics are a very powerful way to get children more involved with both music and poetry.

This activity revolves around a game which is great fun and can be played with any age children. Tell the class that you are going to read out some lyrics to a song, as if they were a poem, and the children have to guess the song. Put the class into teams of four or five and give them a 'buzzer' or bell which they need to press/ring when they think they know the answer. Begin with an easy one, for example 'All Things Bright and Beautiful', but perhaps start mid-song, for example 'Each little flower that opens, each little bird that sings, He made their glowing colours, He made their tiny wings'. If a group knows the answer, they get one point; if they can sing the song, they get a bonus point.

Popular music is great to use, because these songs often sound very different when they are read as poetry. Choose chart hits that children are likely to be familiar with. Children can then begin to create their own quiz questions, choosing favourite songs and reading these as if they were poems, to the class. This activity will involve plenty of listening to music, recording lyrics and accessing a wide range of vocabulary – powerful indeed!

Activity 3: Poetic movement

This activity relates to the example described earlier in the chapter, where Babcock (2016) brought haiku and dance together in a five-year project. This would be a wonderful way to make connections across the curriculum and has the potential to develop the many skills that Babcock noticed her students acquiring.

Talk to children about haiku poems and how the aim is to capture the absolute essence of something in very few words. Read some examples and give children time to explore and perhaps write some of their own. Choose an example which has the potential for promoting movement and dance – sometimes it is better to write your own so that you have a resource that best suits the children you teach and your lesson aims. I have written the following:

Storm
Leaves shake free of trees
Animals run to ground
A storm approaches
(Virginia Bower)

I wrote this haiku very deliberately, with movement being at the heart of the poem. First, there is the movement of the leaves, then the animals, then the incoming storm. Dance moves could be explored which reflect these movements, perhaps putting children into groups, each group to explore possibilities for each line. If you have already been following a dance scheme they will probably have plenty of ideas, but if this is new to you or them, there are some useful short videos – mini-workouts – on YouTube which might give children some initial ideas – www.youtube.com/watch?v=z7tbdF6l SKO&list=PLC2C841486EB885F1&index=1.

Once children have their dance moves decided and practised, they can put their 'lines of dance' together for a performance. This could be recorded so that they can later evaluate the performance and decide whether they think it represents the haiku in an effective way. Hopefully the children will now be ready to have a go at the whole process, including writing their own haiku poems as a starting point. They might want to think in reverse order – which type of dance moves do they prefer – rhythmical, sharp and staccato, smooth and relaxing, energetic and dynamic. They can then choose subject matter for their haiku which will suit their dance style preferences. Alternatively, they can write the haiku first, as in my example, and then fit the dance moves to their poem. To make for a further challenge, they might write haiku poems for each other and then provide feedback on how their haikus have been interpreted through dance. Lots of possibilities here and this might seem quite daunting if you have not taught a great deal of dance or poetry before. Just give it a go and you will find the children soon lead the way and leave you to watch and enjoy!

Activity 4: Freeze that verse!

Freeze frames are a great pedagogical tool to use across the curriculum and you can bring so many aspects of learning together here – drama, poetry and any curriculum subject. This activity uses the poem, 'Night Flight' by Laura Mucha, which you can find here – https://childrens.poetryarchive.org/poem/night-flight/. This poem could be linked with the theme of day and night, or the sky at night, or different views of our towns and cities – common themes that occur across the curriculum for different key stages.

Read the poem to the children or play the recording by the poet at the link above (preferably do both, so that children really become acquainted with the ideas in the poem). You could then divide the class into five groups and they could each recite a stanza and then all join in for the final line. By this time, they should know the poem very well and you can move onto the drama element. Discuss freeze frames with the children if they are not already familiar with these. If you need a reminder yourself, the website 'Drama Resource' set up by David Farmer is very useful – https://dramaresource.com/freeze-frames/.

Explain to the children that they are going to produce a freeze frame to represent their stanza. Give children time to work on this and then, as you play the recording of the poem, each group goes into their freeze frame as their part of the poem is recited. Record this and then play the video to the children, pausing on each freeze frame so that they can analyse and evaluate how effective each one is in relation to representing their stanzas. Discuss why some stanzas were more difficult to represent than others. This should provoke some interesting discussions about the subject matter of the poems and the vocabulary used. In this way, deeper learning is taking place. Try this activity with other poems – different poetic forms, a range of subject matter, rhyming and non-rhyming. You will get different responses each time and children will be making connections across subjects and genres and will gain a deeper understanding of the poems they read.

References

Anderson, J. (2010) On the Move: Poetry and Dance, *Dance Chronicle*, 33, 2, 251–267.

Armstrong, J. (2013) *Combining Poetry with Visual Art to See (and Feel) in a New Way*, Available at: www.moma.org/explore/inside_out/2013/10/16/combining-poetry-with-visual-art-to-see-and-feel-in-a-new-way/. Accessed on 03.02.2022.

Athanases, Z. (2005) 'Performing the Drama of the Poem: Workshop, Rehearsal, and Reflection', *The English Journal*, 95, 1, 88–96.

Babcock, M. L. (2016) 'Merging Dance with Poetry through Collaborative Learning: Exploring Classroom Practices Studying Improvisation as a Tool for Choreography', *Journal of Modern Education Review*, 6, 2, 125–134.

Besner, L. (2012) 'Why We Should Treat Poetry Like Painting'. Available at: https://hazlitt.net/feature/why-we-should-treat-poetry-painting. Accessed on 09.02.2021.

Britannica (no date) *The Arts*. Available at: www.britannica.com/topic/the-arts. Accessed on 03.02.2022.

CLPE (2017) *Evaluation of the Centre for Literacy in Primary Education (CLPE) Power of Poetry Training Programme*, London: CLPE.

Ferguson, K. (2014) *Performing Poetry: Using Drama to Increase the Comprehension of Poetry*, What Works? Research into Practice, Research Monograph 52, Ontario: Literacy and Numeracy Secretariat and the Ontario Association of Deans of Education.

Graham, L. & Johnson, A. (2012) *Children's Writing Journals*, Leicester: UKLA.

Jusslin, S. & Höglund, H. (2021) 'Arts-based Responses to Teaching Poetry: A Literature Review of Dance and Visual Arts in Poetry Education', *Literacy*, 55, 1, 39–51.

Kleppe, S. L. (2018) 'Teaching Poetry with Painting: "Why Do You Thus Devise Evil Against Her?"', in Kleppe, S. L. & Sorby, A. (eds.), *Poetry and Pedagogy Across the Lifespan: Disciplines, Classrooms and Contexts*, London: Palgrave Macmillan, 73–94.

National Public Radio (2006) 'Leonard Cohen on Poetry, Music and Why He Left the Zen Monastery'. Available at: www.npr.org/2016/10/21/498810429/leonard-cohen-on-poetry-music-and-why-he-left-the-zen-monastery?t=1644148849945. Accessed on 06.02.2022.

Paton, G. (2014) 'Nicky Morgan: Pupils "Held Back" By Overemphasis on Arts', *The Telegraph*. Available at: www.telegraph.co.uk/education/educationnews/11221081/Nicky-Morgan-pupils-held-back-by-overemphasis-on-arts.html. Accessed 07.02.2022.

Poetry Foundation (no date) 'Poetry and Music'. Available at: www.poetryfoundation.org/collections/148663/poetry-and-music. Accessed on 09.02.2022.

Ruck Keene, H. (2020) 'The Arts as Handmaiden', in Bower, V. (ed.), *Debates in Primary Education*, Abingdon: Routledge, 107–124.

Webb, J. (2017) 'What's in a Name? Writing Across Borders of Poetry and Music', *The Conversation*. Available at: https://theconversation.com/whats-in-a-name-writing-across-borders-of-poetry-and-music-79669. Accessed on 09.02.2022.

Wheeler, B. (2016) *Can Song Lyrics Ever Be Poetry?* Available at: www.bbc.com/news/magazine-37637797. Accessed on 09.02.2022.

10 Poetry for physical and mental health and wellbeing

We would all like to think that children's physical and mental health are at the forefront of decision making in school – whether this be to do with curriculum, pedagogy or assessment. However, in an age of accountability, surveillance and the questioning of our professional judgements and decisions, this is not always straightforward. This chapter provides ideas on how poetry can be embedded in everyday practice to support children's – and indeed our own – physical and mental health. Health is a vast topic and I have therefore chosen, in the first section of this chapter, to look specifically at physical *activity* and the connections between physical activity and learning, and how poetry can become an effective part of this. This includes a focus on embodied cognition. I then move on to examine the ways in which poetry can support children's (and our own) positive mental health and wellbeing, bringing in examples of powerful poems that might be utilised.

Introduction

As practitioners, the physical and mental health and wellbeing of our pupils is always at the forefront of our minds, whatever role we hold. However, this is not so easy to promote in an age of accountability, surveillance and the questioning of our professional judgements and decisions. It might be that the physical education lesson we had planned, where children were going to have time to explore movement and body actions, whilst collaborating and working in teams, is jettisoned because another area of the curriculum is perceived to need more time – perhaps because of an upcoming assessment. It might be that part way through a science lesson, a child mentions something that is calling out for further discussion; something which might be baffling the child, or they are seeking clarification. However, we look at our watch and, concerned with the need to cover the outlined objective of the lesson, we let the child's comment pass and move on. Maybe you are not party to this type of incident; all I know is that I certainly was when I was working in a primary school setting, mainly because of the pressures on curriculum time.

As I hope I have indicated through all the other chapters, poetry is our ally in all this and can come to the rescue! By embedding poetry across the curriculum and using the spaces and moments of our school day, we can make up for those instants where we do lose sight of what should be our primary objective – the positive mental and physical health of our pupils, colleagues and, of course, ourselves.

DOI: 10.4324/9781003154174-11

In terms of health and wellbeing, writing poetry can help us engage more physically and mentally with different environments, using our senses to explore and express feelings. It can allow us to visit places in our mind which might not easily be explored in any other way; find a way to say things we struggle to voice. Reading poems, or being read to, allows children to recognise their own emotions and hear about these from others' perspectives; to realise that it is perfectly acceptable to feel the way they do – potentially the first step to being able to deal with difficult feelings, thoughts and emotions.

Physical health is an extensive topic and I have chosen therefore, in the first section of this chapter, to look specifically at physical *activity* and the connections between physical activity and learning, and how poetry can become an effective part of this. This includes a focus on embodied cognition. I then move on to examine the ways in which poetry can support children's (and our own) positive mental health and wellbeing, bringing in examples of powerful poems that might be utilised. The chapter concludes with two practical activities focusing on physical activity and poetry and two centred around mental health, wellbeing and poetry.

Physical activity, learning and poetry

This section begins by examining the links between physical activity, learning and poetry, introducing 'embodied cognition', a concept which has emerged largely since the turn of the century. I then go on to more practical application of these ideas, examining how we might use poetry to promote physical activity and the benefits of this in terms of both physical health and children's learning.

Embodied cognition

If we are to argue for a higher status for physical activity in our educational settings; to persuade curriculum designers, senior leaders in schools, teachers, parents and children that physical activity needs to be a priority, evidence from research indicating links between physical activity and learning is totally pertinent. But what must follow are pedagogies that allow for practical application in the classroom; pedagogies that support active learning, with children spending far less time in their seats as passive receivers of knowledge. Poetry can be a significant resource in this.

So, first, the research. A good place to start is with 'embodied cognition' as this concept reflects some of the more recent work emerging from neuroscience. To put it simply, embodied cognition is learning enhanced by action. Neuroscientific studies suggest 'a tight connection between cognitive processing and brain areas associated with physical motion' (Shapiro and Stolz, 2019, p. 24). For example, if we were to read something about people dancing in the streets, areas of the brain would activate which relate to being actively and personally involved with dancing.

Embodied cognition denies the idea that body and mind are disconnected; that anything intellectual is the domain of the mind and anything practical is the domain of the body. Instead, the mind, the body and the environment all work together, leading to learning (see Figure 10.1), and 'the body plays a central role in shaping the mind' (Kosmas, 2018, p. 970).

Poetry for physical and mental health and wellbeing 123

Figure 10.1 Embodied cognition (adapted from the ideas of Shapiro and Stolz [2019])

Skipping rhymes and engaging with skipping or 'jump rope' provide a perfect exemplar of this interaction between the mind, body and environment. The rhyme itself provides the stimulus and children need to learn each rhyme 'by heart' in order to participate (cognitive engagement). Skipping as an activity by itself is well known to be a beneficial cardiac workout and calorie burner (Bottoms, 2020) (active body) and is also a real challenge in terms of developing motor skills. Engaging in skipping games involves mediation within the environment – social interaction, choices to be made, rules to be communicated, decisions acted upon and the development of emotional resilience within the possibility of failure. And what of the poetry in all of this? Throughout the playing of skipping games comes immersion in rhythm, rhyme, alliteration and other poetic features that children will meet in more 'formal' contexts. The aspects of poetry that occur in their skipping games build a bridge to easier access when exploring more challenging poetry and, rather than shying away from this challenge, children can bring to it their own memories and experiences.

You can find ten popular skipping rhymes here – www.skip-hop.co.uk/top-ten-skipping-rhymes/ – or there is a useful booklet of skipping rhymes which you could print out for children, and it has a space for them to write their own at the end – www.cne-siar.gov.uk/media/5254/skipping-rhymes-booklet.pdf. Here is a classic example to get you started:

Tiny Tim
I had a little puppy
His name was Tiny Tim
I put him in the bathtub, to see if he could swim
He drank all the water, he ate a bar of soap
The next thing you know he had a bubble in his throat.
In came the doctor, (person jumps in)
In came the nurse, (person jumps in)
In came the lady with the alligator purse (person jumps in)
Out went the doctor (person jumps out)
Out went the nurse (person jumps out)
Out went the lady with the alligator purse (person jumps out)

Returning to the discussion around embodied cognition, Shapiro and Stolz (2019, p. 27) go on to write that, when a person successfully completes a task, 'it may appear that they are dependent on sophisticated cognitive operations, when in fact they are exploiting features of the environment in a way that reduces cognitive load'. I would argue that, by promoting activities such as skipping games, we are sowing the seeds for reducing the cognitive load when it comes to more challenging learning. Children can draw on their intrinsic knowledge of poetic features (absorbed through skipping games), to reduce the cognitive load and allow for, potentially, other lines of thought and their opinions to emerge relating to poems that demand interpretation.

An interesting example, involving a different type of physical activity, comes from a project undertaken nearly 30 years ago, by Boswell and Mentzer (1995). They organised what they called 'The Movement Poetry Program' with primary age children who had issues with behaviour and what was then referred to as Attention Deficit Disorder (ADD). The idea was to introduce movement into lessons, with the aim of increasing children's interest in and appreciation of poetry whilst also releasing excess energy and tension. The lessons involved reading a poem to the children and then asking a series of questions, which would be increasingly challenging, to reflect the ideas in the poem. The students were required to respond in a physical way, for example: Can you shake your head? Can you shake other parts of your body? Can you shake one part and keep the other parts still? Can you shake one part quickly and another part slowly? Boswell and Mentzer found that there was an increase in positive interactions with peers, opportunities to release energy and tension and a better understanding of concepts in the poems. Although at this time the idea of 'embodied cognition' was only just emerging, the findings of this project reflect much of what is highlighted as the benefits of taking into account the relationship between mind, body and environment.

Shapiro and Stolz (2019) suggest two key challenges with any kind of learning in classrooms. First, concepts tend to be 'delivered' to children without reference or access to an original source. An example might be teaching English children about the flora and fauna in Africa. The children cannot (generally) go to Africa and they are gaining their information from 'secondhand knowledge' (ibid., p. 27), having to build up their knowledge and understanding in this way. However, the second challenge highlighted that having the actual experience can also be problematic 'because direct experiences need to be coupled with secondhand knowledge to be given any meaning' (ibid.). This is where poems can be a powerful bridge between what Shapiro and Stolz describe as the 'original referent' and 'secondhand knowledge', as they allow glimpses into different places and lives without the need for a didactic, teacher-led approach. The next section looks at how this can all come together, to promote physical activity, an enjoyment of poetry and cognitive development.

Using poetry to promote physical activity

With poetry and physical activity, the learning is a constant two-way shift. If used effectively, the poetry improves children's experience of physical activity and the physical activity improves their understanding of poetry. An example might be in dance where, through a series of dance moves, children can gain a better understanding of specific language used in a poem. Access Jacob Sam-La Rose's poem 'A Life in Dreams' on the Poetry Archive website: https://childrens.poetryarchive.org/poem/a-life-in-dreams/.

In this poem, Jacob evokes images, sounds, feelings which might take us to places that we too have visited in our dreams. Some of the ideas are immediately accessible and I think children will relate easily to them. Others are more complex. Stanza 2 for example, might resonate with children's experiences of particular dreams, where it feels like they cannot move or run from an unnamed threat. However, they might not immediately comprehend all of the vocabulary, and this would be a wonderful chance to explore the ideas through dance and movement.

Ask children to create moves that show them attempting to move through the 'treacle' yet fail to move very far at all. They can exaggerate and repeat the moves, perhaps working in pairs to choreograph some steps. Other pairs could work on dance moves that reveal them as the hidden threat – the ogre of the dream, edging closer. The pairs could then come together, combining their dance moves (perhaps with some sinister music) and creating a brief performance. There then needs to be time to revisit the poem and focus on that particular stanza. What meaning does it have now? Remember, there are no correct answers – just a chance to discuss and share ideas and perhaps, for you, to assess their developing comprehension of words and concepts.

In Bessell and Riddell's (2016) research, they provide an example relating to a group of dancers who were asked to use a sonnet as the starting point for some choreography, and it was noted that, as they allocated each part of the poem a 'physical commitment' (ibid.) their ability to memorise the poem in a short period of time was significant. Bessell and Riddell (2016, p. 327) write that 'when participants are encouraged to put a movement to a poem that they are learning, the learning is assisted', and I think this is not just about learning a poem by heart, but learning more about how the poem speaks to you as an individual and what it means to you. This seems to demonstrate the two-way effect I mentioned earlier, where the poem provides the dance inspiration, and the dance enhances access to the poem. It is also an example of embodied cognition, as discussed earlier in the chapter.

The research indicated that 'in order to understand a poem fully, it is necessary not only to interpret the meanings of both concrete and abstract words, but also to respond to the sentiment behind the words' (ibid., p. 332) and the embodiment of these sentiments, through dance, may have supported this understanding. If you work with early years children and are thinking that this is beyond the capabilities of very young children, do not be deterred – we need to start this approach as early as possible! It is all about the choice of poem, the modelling provided and the freedom to interpret – then children will run with it! There is a great poem to get you started with young children called 'Watery Workout' by Gershon Wolf, which you can access here – www.poetrysoup.com/poem/watery_workout_1172527.

To a certain extent, in this section, I have implicitly included reference to how physical activity and poetry can undoubtedly also promote positive *mental* health and wellbeing, particularly when we consider the linked aspects of embodied cognition – mind, body, environment. The next section however will explore mental health and wellbeing more explicitly, and how poems can be a part of promoting this.

Mental health, wellbeing and poetry

In this section, I begin by examining some general connections between positive mental health and poetry and how the reading and writing of poetry can be one way to promote a classroom with its foundations rooted in positive pedagogy. I then move onto a specific feature of some poems – rhythm and rhyme – and the significant beneficial effects of these on our mental health and wellbeing.

The links between positive mental health, wellbeing and poetry

Considerable research has been undertaken to explore the links between positive mental health and wellbeing and poetry. If you are interested in reading some of these studies, the International Arts and Mind (IAM) website – www.artsandmindlab.org/more-than-words-why-poetry-is-good-for-our-health/ – makes reference to several and provides the necessary links. It is so good to see the research into this area, as it further validates the use of poetry across the curriculum, highlighting myriad positive effects. The IAM organisation reports that there are aspects of poetry which can reassure and ease our minds, particularly if we are suffering from stress or bereavement or trauma (IAM, no date). It might be the rhythm and meter of a poem; it could be the words used by the poet; it might be the images conveyed which speak to us and allow us to make sense of our own and others' lives.

In a study which used poetry with hospitalised children to ascertain whether the reading and writing of poetry would impact on their emotional wellbeing, the researchers found that there were 'statistically significant reductions in fear, sadness, anger, worry, and fatigue' (Delamerced et al., 2021) and most of the children felt happy after the poetry activities. The IAM organisation report on other studies which indicate that poetry writing sessions support teenagers suffering from depression and trauma; that therapy involving poetry has positive impacts on the mental health of cancer patients; and that those who are in caring professions benefit from poetry therapy.

Whilst it is extremely valuable to consider the therapeutic effects of poetry on those who might be struggling with their mental health, it is also important to consider how poems can *promote* wellbeing – a proactive as opposed to a reactive approach. Croom (2014) uses Seligman's (2011) characteristic components of psychological wellbeing – positive emotion, engagement, relationships, meaning and accomplishment – to analyse how poetry can have a positive effect on mental health. He draws on a range of studies indicating that poetry can provoke *positive emotion* and can allow for those engaged with poetry to enter a state of 'flow' – 'the experience of complete absorption in the present moment' (Nakamura and Csikszentmihalyi, 2009, p. 195, cited in Croom, 2014) – also associated with persistence, resilience and improved self-esteem. Not all poems will induce this state of flow, but if we are developing reading habits that include poetry, children will begin to find examples that 'speak' to them. This might be as a result of the rhythm or rhyme (see further discussion later in the chapter), the way a poem is read or the use of vocabulary that draws us in.

When I think of flow, I remember my mother reading Belloc's 'Tarantella' to me at bedtime and I suspect I was in a state of flow listening to the rhythms and cadences of this wonderful poem. Take a look at the poem and have a go at reading it aloud and you may see what I mean:

Tarantella

Do you remember an Inn,
Miranda?
Do you remember an Inn?
And the tedding and the spreading
Of the straw for a bedding,
And the fleas that tease in the High Pyrenees,

And the wine that tasted of tar?
And the cheers and the jeers of the young muleteers
(Under the vine of the dark verandah)?
Do you remember an Inn, Miranda,
Do you remember an Inn?
And the cheers and the jeers of the young muleteeers
Who hadn't got a penny,
And who weren't paying any,
And the hammer at the doors and the Din?
And the Hip! Hop! Hap!
Of the clap
Of the hands to the twirl and the swirl
Of the girl gone chancing,
Glancing,
Dancing,
Backing and advancing,
Snapping of a clapper to the spin
Out and in –
And the Ting, Tong, Tang, of the Guitar.
Do you remember an Inn,
Miranda?
Do you remember an Inn?
Never more;
Miranda,
Never more.
Only the high peaks hoar:
And Aragon a torrent at the door.
No sound
In the walls of the Halls where falls
The tread
Of the feet of the dead to the ground
No sound:
But the boom
Of the far Waterfall like Doom.

(Hillaire Beloc)

Croom (2014) moves on to examine the third of Seligman's components of psychological well-being – *relationships* – and again finds much evidence from research to suggest that poetry is a powerful resource for supporting the development of strong relationships. He uses the example of spoken word and performance poetry, which brings people together from different backgrounds, sometimes at large, national events; at other times in small, intimate settings. Although this type of event would be possible to set up within or between schools, it is unlikely to be a regular occurrence in primary settings. What is perhaps more pertinent is the point Croom makes about poetry being able to connect us to others; through hearing about lives and experiences expressed through poems, we gain an insight which supports us with the development of our own relationships and dealings with others. This connects smoothly with Seligman's fourth component – *meaning* – as, through poetry, children can begin to see life from different perspectives and to make better sense of the different worlds they inhabit – home, school, places they visit and so forth.

Finally, Croom examines 'accomplishment' as a component of psychological wellbeing and how poetry can support accomplishment, achievement and self-esteem. Through poetry, children can hear the voices of others and find their own; they can be immersed in vocabulary that enables more effective communication of ideas; and they can experience freedom within which to develop their ideas. All of these have the potential to impact on children's accomplishments, both in and outside the classroom.

On the Power Poetry (no date) website, they refer to 'mental wellness' and discuss five reasons why and how this wellness can be promoted through the writing of poetry. If we link these reasons to the components discussed above, a powerful argument emerges for using poetry to promote mental health and wellbeing. I will look briefly at each of the reasons presented. First, the authors on the Power Poetry site talk about the freedom that can be gained from poetry writing; having the opportunity to write about anything you wish and to use it as a way of releasing feelings and emotions or asking questions. They also explore the idea that writing poetry provokes honesty and introspection; we can look at our lives, our thoughts, feelings and opinions and then put these on paper, which in turn enables us to understand ourselves and our motivations. With this is mind, there is a wonderful poem by Laura Mucha called 'The Land of Blue' – https://childrens.poetryarchive.org/poem/the-land-of-the-blue/ – which would be a powerful resource to use with all age children. The poet explores the idea that we all have 'blue' moments but that 'the golden skies' are on the other side and, by recognising this, we better understand ourselves and the actions of others.

Whilst acknowledging the usefulness of exploring emotions through poems, the authors from Power Poetry also refer to the utility of metaphor in poetry so that we do not necessarily have to refer to ourselves directly and can approach difficult or sensitive subjects through figurative devices which allow for a certain distance when necessary. There is a very powerful poem by Andrew Fusek-Peters and Polly Peters called 'Bruises Heal' – https://childrens.poetryarchive.org/poem/bruises-heal/ – which is suitable for older children, where the poets make effective use of metaphor – 'Her words are scalpels' and 'Laughter slices' – and using this with children would give them an idea of how metaphor can be used to convey strong messages.

The article on the Power Poetry website then moves on to examine how poems allow us to tell our stories – 'an empowering act that makes you feel validated and heard' – and this of course is so important for all the children we teach – to provide opportunities for them to have a voice (I explore this in more depth in Chapter 1). But it is not all about our own voices of course; listening to poems by others that tell stories about lives, places, events and so forth, enables us all to feel part of a wider world, connected, belonging; to feel a responsibility towards others. Takolander (2021) writes that 'Poetry, representative of emotion, is also frequently used to symbolise humanity' and if we are to build a more sustainable future, our children need to know what it is to be both human and humane; to empathise with and have compassion for others. This in turn has a positive effect on wellbeing and regular exposure to poems can play a significant role here.

There is a wonderful poem by Kit Wright called 'In Memory of a Beautiful Jeweller' – https://childrens.poetryarchive.org/poem/in-memory-of-a-beautiful-jeweller/ – which is full of imagery and humanity and love and is ideal to explore with older children. For younger children, Andrew Fusek-Peters' kenning poem 'Mum' is underpinned by love and appreciation – https://childrens.poetryarchive.org/poem/mum-polly-peters/ – and an ideal text to illustrate, even with very young learners, how we can use poetry to 'symbolise humanity'.

The final aspect discussed on the Power Poetry site is the way that poetry can allow us to write explicitly about specific aspects of mental health: anxiety, depression, fear and lack of self-esteem. In so doing, we bring into the open subjects that might otherwise be difficult to broach or discuss with others. This type of poem may not be appropriate for early years and primary age children to read but they are good for us, as practitioners, to allow an insight into how others feel and to perhaps recognise when we need to focus on our own health and wellbeing. There are some powerful examples here – https://happiful.com/7-poems-that-teach-us-about-mental-health/.

Hopefully this has given you some idea of the power of poetry when we consider the mental health and wellbeing of our pupils and ourselves. Before finishing this section, I want to explore in a little more depth the idea that specific features of poems – that perhaps occur with more regularity within this genre than in others – can have a positive effect on mental health and wellbeing.

Features of poetry that promote positive mental health

Research indicates that rhythm and rhyme can have particularly beneficial effects, in terms of mental health and wellbeing. This could be for a number of reasons. Arguably, poems with a strong rhythm and rhyme allow easier access to the genre. With poems that rhyme, the end word of lines can often be predicted and, in terms of children learning to read or developing their comprehension strategies, this can provide a powerful scaffold (see Chapter 3 for more discussion on this). If we think back to the earlier discussion on embodied cognition there is the suggestion that physical activity can – in one way or another – lessen the cognitive load in one area, thereby providing space for new or deeper learning in other areas. In this case, rhythm and rhyme can lighten this load and in turn can allow children to enjoy and feel confident with accessing this genre, empowered to give voice to their opinions and eager to listen to the views of others.

Research also suggests that features of poetry can trigger emotional responses. A study undertaken by Obermeier et al. (2013, p. 8), found that meter and rhythm in poems had an impact on 'aesthetic and emotional responses to poetry' and in particular, when there was a regular rhythm and rhyme, 'heightened aesthetic appreciation and intensity of processing as well as more positive emotional responses' occurred. Menninghaus et al. (2017, p. 55) found that when participants experienced 'sadly moving' or 'joyfully moving' poems containing rhyme, rhythm and alliteration, there were 'higher ratings for sadness, being moved, joy, intensity, and positive affect'.

I have highlighted just two examples here of how poetic features can influence learning and wellbeing, but there are assuredly others and you might want to consider what these are, as you explore poems with the children you teach. This power over our emotions, evoked by certain poems, is something to treasure as a classroom resource, always being aware of the care needed to appreciate that each and every poem will mean something different to the reader and may provoke a whole range of emotions.

Activities

Activity 1: Exploring movement through poetry

This activity can be used in many different ways. It could be a great warm-up for a physical education lesson; it could be part of a series of dance lessons, gradually choreographing a sequence for a performance; it might be part of your English lesson, where, to really get 'inside' the poem, you plan in time for movement and enacting the poem, putting 'embodied cognition' into action! However, as this chapter is focused on poetry and physical and mental health, the specific ideas in this activity are related to how you might combine poetry and dance.

Before your planned dance lesson, access the poem entitled 'The Windy Day' by visiting www.kidspoetryclub.com/poems-about-weather (you will also find some useful podcasts and activities to use with your class on this site). Read the poem at least twice (volunteers could read a stanza each or as a group perhaps). You could have some recorded sounds of wind blowing in the background to enhance the atmosphere. Explain to the children that, during the dance lesson, they are going to design movements for the poem, to tell the poet's 'story'. If you wanted, you could allocate each group a particular part of the poem and then join the sections together at the end.

I would avoid giving the children too many ideas – allow them to interpret the poem in their own ways. Provide plenty of time for getting to know the poem well, discussion, planning, rehearsing and performing – it will be worth it! A recording of the final performance could be made, with a voice-over of the poem being read.

Activity 2: Poetry in the playground

Children lead this activity – with their knowledge, experience, active bodies and active minds. Start by asking them to work in groups and discuss any playground activities that involve rhymes and songs. These might be clapping or skipping games, individual, paired or group activities. Ask each group to share their examples and make a list of these. Explain to the class that they are going to go onto the playground and show their games to their own group and then to other groups. Plenty of time is needed for this, so that all the children learn new rhymes and games and can practise and play with different members of the class. You may well be outside all morning or afternoon! I hope so!

If you have time the same day (or, even better, leave the next morning free), spend time asking children which were their favourites and why. Were any similar to those you were already aware of? Where did you learn these rhymes and games? Discuss the rhyme and rhythm which is typical of this genre. How are playground rhymes different to other poems? *Are* they different?

Choose a well know playground rhyme – this could be an example from a class member or from the website mentioned earlier in the chapter. Explain that, as a shared writing exercise, you are going to personalise this rhyme, to make it relevant to the class – perhaps changing names, activities and so on. Take some time to learn this new version and then return to the playground to put it into action. A collection of playground rhymes can be put together – on paper or digitally – and this could be shared with other classes, who might then add their versions.

Activity 3: Happy thoughts

In this activity, the children will produce one couplet each, relating to happiness. With only two lines to focus on, all the children should be able to produce their own mini poems. If you are working with early years children or Key Stage 1, you could do this as a whole class or group activity, collecting ideas and scribing for them.

Read 'Happy Thought' by Robert Louis Stevenson:

> The world is so full of a number of things
> I'm sure we should all be as happy as kings.

Pose some questions: What do you think Stevenson was thinking about when he wrote 'a number of things'? What would you say are the things that make you happy? Give the children time to work in pairs to share three things that make them happy.

Explain to the children that they are going to write their own 'Happy Thoughts' poem – just two lines long in either the form of a rhyming couplet or two non-rhyming lines.

Model two examples – one rhyming and one non-rhyming. Here are two of mine:

> Summer holidays, sand and sea
> This is what happiness means to me.
> (Virginia Bower)

> The first day of a holiday
> Everything to come.
> (Virginia Bower)

Using the ideas they shared earlier in the session, children then work in pairs to produce their happy thoughts poems. These would make a wonderful display and, at another time you could perhaps share 'sad thoughts' or 'excited thoughts' or 'worried thoughts' and poems could be written to reflect these. Earlier in the chapter I wrote about the power of poetry to allow for release of emotions and, carefully conducted, this could be a powerful, ongoing exercise.

Activity 4: Exploring emotions

Give children the line 'I'm so excited I could…' and ask them to work in pairs to come up with different endings to the line. Model an example, e.g. 'I'm so excited my toes are trying to escape my feet!' Ask them to write their ideas on post-it notes and to stick them onto a flipchart at the front of the classroom (if you are working with younger children, they could share their ideas verbally with you and you write them on the board). Organise the post-its into a vertical arrangement and read the ideas to the class, as a list poem. Talk to them about this being one way to gather ideas about emotions and that we all have a range of emotions at different times, triggered by different experiences.

Share a range of poems concerned with feelings and emotions. You could use Colin McNaughton's 'Mum Is Having a Baby' – https://carrypaterson.wordpress.com/2015/09/09/mom-is-having-a-baby/ – or my poem below. Even better, write your own to share!

Joy
Joy
Is a leaping gazelle
Crossing the mind's meadows in a single bound
Limitless possibilities
The whole world
Awaits
(Virginia Bower)

Group tables in the classroom so that each table has a 'feeling' or 'emotion', for example anger, joy, sadness, loneliness, fear. Have at least six poems for each table. Ask the children to choose a feeling/emotion and move to the relevant table (choice is important here) and read the poems either with others or on their own (support from adults can be provided where necessary, although this should ideally be kept for supporting reading the poems, rather than influencing ideas and opinions). Ask children to gather vocabulary from the poems which reflect the emotions in effective ways. Share all the vocabulary to create an 'emotion list'. This can then be used in future poetry writing activities or across the curriculum when children are discussing feelings and emotions.

References

Bessell, J. & Riddell, P. (2016) 'Embodiment and Performance', *Changing English*, 23, 4, 326-334.
Boswell, B. B. & Mentzer, M. (1995) 'Integrating Poetry and Movement for Children with Learning and/or Behavioural Disabilities, *Intervention in School and Clinic*, 31, 2, 108-113.

Bottoms, L. (2020) 'Grab a Rope: Seven Reasons Why Skipping Is So Good for You', *The Conversation*. Available at: https://theconversation.com/grab-a-rope-seven-reasons-why-skipping-is-so-good-for-you-144649. Accessed on 15.02.2022.

Croom, A. M. (2014) 'The Practice of Poetry and the Psychology of Well-being', *Journal of Poetry Therapy*, 28, 1, 21-41.

Delamerced, A., Panicker, C., Monteiro, K. & Chung, E. Y. (2021) 'Effects of a Poetry Intervention on Emotional Wellbeing in Hospitalized Pediatric Patients', *Hospital Pediatrics*, 11, 3, 263-269.

International Arts and Mind (IAM) (no date) *More Than Words: Why Poetry Is Good for Our Health*. Available at: International Arts + Mind Lab: The Center for Applied Neuroaesthetics, artsandmindlab.org. Accessed on 15.02.2022.

Kosmas, P. (2018) 'Embodied Cognition and Its Implications in Education: An Overview of Recent Literature', *World Academy of Science, Engineering and Technology International Journal of Educational and Pedagogical Sciences*, 12, 7, 970-976.

Menninghaus, W., Wagner, V., Wassiliwizky, E., Jacobsen, T. & Knoop, C. A. (2017) 'The Emotional and Aesthetic Powers of Parallelistic Diction', *Poetics*, 63, 47-59.

Nakamura, J. & Csikszentmihalyi, M. (2009) 'Flow Theory and Research', in Lopez, S. & Snyder, C. R. (eds.), *Oxford Handbook of Positive Psychology*, Oxford: Oxford University Press, 195-206.

Obermeier, C., Menninghaus, W., von Koppenfels, M., Raettig, T., Schmidt-Kassow, M., Otterbein, S. & Kotz, S. A. (2013) 'Aesthetic and Emotional Effects of Meter and Rhyme in Poetry', *Frontiers in Psychology*, 4, 1-10.

Power Poetry (no date) *Use Poetry to Maintain Mental Wellness*. Available at: Use Poetry to Maintain Mental Wellness | Power Poetry, https://powerpoetry.org/actions/use-poetry-maintain-mental-wellness. Accessed on 15.02.2022.

Seligman, M. E. P. (2011) *Flourish: A Visionary New Understanding of Happiness and Well-being*, New York: Free Press.

Shapiro, L. & Stolz, S. A. (2019) 'Embodied Cognition and Its Significance for Education', *Theory and Research in Education*, 17, 1, 19-39.

Takolander, M. (2021) 'Moved by Words: How Poetry Helps Us Express Our Feelings', *The Conversation*. Available at: https://theconversation.com/moved-by-words-how-poetry-helps-us-express-our-feelings-161892. Accessed on 15.02.2022.

INDEX

accountability 3-4, 7, 9, 11, 17, 21, 24, 35, 97, 121
aesthetic/s 9, 16, 21, 69, 70, 72, 82, 95, 111, 129, 133
agency 50, 52, 97, 109
alliteration 60, 123, 129
analyse 4, 6, 16, 120, 126
anthology/ies 12-13, 67, 112
articulate 2, 14, 22, 25, 59-60, 73, 110
artwork 87, 110-11, 117-18
assess 3, 5, 24, 44, 98, 105, 125
assessment 3, 5, 7, 9, 33, 40-1, 68, 91, 97, 116, 121
audience 25-6, 103
audio 14, 31, 38, 41, 44, 47, 54, 66-7, 103-4, 111, 114
authentic 15, 29, 48-9, 69-70, 91, 98, 102

beauty 1-2, 23, 59, 64, 72, 77, 79, 81, 94
blog 18, 76, 78, 106, 111

cadence 1, 15, 25, 47, 50, 52, 103, 126
canon 3, 5, 25
catalyst 3, 18, 46-7, 74-5
choral 13, 27-8, 33, 89, 115-16
cognates 8, 58-60, 62
collaboration 15, 44, 98-9, 114
collaborative 5, 38, 56, 99, 106, 114, 120
collocation 8, 58-61, 68
community/ies 58-9, 63-4, 74, 83, 85-7, 94-5, 98, 104, 106, 114
comprehension 5, 8, 34-6, 39-45, 62, 85, 115-16, 120, 125, 129
connecting curriculum 7, 11-12, 14-15
constraints 9-10, 69, 78
counting 9, 36, 69, 76-9
creative 1, 9, 18, 21, 33, 47, 57, 69-74, 82, 84, 86, 95, 98-100, 108-20

creativity 3, 69-72, 82, 85-6
culture 3, 7-8, 11, 16, 21, 28, 33, 42, 45, 48, 51, 58-9, 64-6, 71, 73, 82, 87, 101, 112-13
culturally responsive 4, 10

dance 9, 78, 109-10, 113-20, 124-5, 130
debate/debating 8, 10, 21-3, 26-7, 30-1, 40, 45, 88, 91, 93, 95, 99, 106-7, 110, 112, 118, 120
decoding 8, 34-45
Development Matters 13, 21, 29, 33, 78, 85, 95
dialogic 26, 32-3
digital 9, 97-108, 131
discipline 2, 7, 9, 69-71, 73, 84, 88, 90, 101, 109, 120
diversity 3, 8, 10, 17, 28, 58-9, 64, 74, 85, 87
drama 9, 27, 109-10, 114-16, 119-20

early years 2-3, 5-6, 9, 11-13, 18-19, 23, 29, 34, 45, 69, 79, 82, 84-6, 98, 106, 110, 113, 125, 129, 131
embodied cognition 10, 38, 121-5, 129-30, 133
emotions 2, 11, 22, 24, 28, 48, 105, 122, 128, 130, 132
empathy 2, 14, 28
engagement 3, 16, 23, 28, 36, 38, 40, 45, 88, 98, 103, 116, 123, 126
English as an additional language (EAL) 48, 59, 81
enquiry 9, 36, 84-5, 87, 90-1
environment 2, 13-14, 19, 52, 74, 86-8, 90, 92-4, 97, 100, 104, 111, 122-5
essence 14, 16, 54-5, 71, 73, 81, 114, 118
ethos 13, 16, 71

foreign 8, 58-61, 67
freedom 40, 49-50, 56, 72, 90, 92, 98, 101, 105, 110, 125, 128

freeze frame 27, 39, 119-20
future 9, 22, 52, 72, 84, 86, 109, 132

games 1, 25, 35, 102, 123, 130-1
genre 3-8, 11-12, 16, 22-3, 28, 34, 46, 48, 50, 60, 89, 98, 102, 129
global 2, 20, 63, 84-6, 95, 98, 103

haiku 17, 51, 54-5, 71, 76, 78, 95, 99, 105-7, 114, 118-19

identity 4, 6, 18, 28, 74
imagery 74-5, 129
imagination 2, 27, 48, 75
impact 4, 12, 16-20, 23-5, 28, 36, 44, 47, 51-2, 60, 77, 79, 84, 86, 91, 103, 113, 115, 126, 128-9
innovation 2, 86, 103
interpretation 10, 16, 20, 22, 26-8, 39-40, 44, 85, 99, 104, 106, 114-16, 124
intonation 26, 76, 103

kenning 49-50, 80-1, 100, 129

learning by heart 8, 22-3, 25, 30, 32
lexical sets 8, 58-62, 81
lexicon 22, 48, 60, 81
linguistic 8, 18, 58-9, 63-4, 68, 101, 112
list 5, 11, 31, 56, 62, 66-7, 81, 93, 100-1, 130, 132
literacy 2-3, 6, 10, 17, 21, 33-4, 45, 57, 97, 101, 107, 113, 120
local 2, 16, 63-4, 84-7, 91-2, 94-5, 98, 103-4
lyric 6, 89-90, 102, 112-13, 118, 120

media 2, 16, 31, 73, 87, 92, 97, 103, 123
memorising 23-4
metaphor/ical 9, 24, 69, 74-5, 80, 83, 87, 91-2, 104, 128
model 8, 16, 21, 29, 44, 46-51, 53, 55-7, 62, 90, 94-5, 99, 103, 106, 117, 125, 131-2
mosaic 2-3, 90, 109
multicultural 8, 58-68
multilingual 8, 58-68
multimodal/ity 9-10, 54, 60, 97-104, 106-8, 115

narrative 3, 26, 29, 90, 92
nature 2, 24, 54, 65, 73, 91, 114-15
non-fiction 3, 34, 47, 85

Ofsted 3, 10, 33, 35, 45, 63
originality 9, 69-72, 82

painting 9, 82, 109-11, 116-17, 120
parents 31, 39, 63, 67, 90, 93, 106, 111, 122
participation 17, 36, 38, 103, 114
patterns 9, 14, 38, 49, 69, 71-2, 76
perform/ing, 78-9, 82, 90, 113
performance 3, 20, 25-8, 31-2, 36, 38-9, 60, 92, 102-3, 111, 114-16, 119, 125, 127, 130, 132
phonics 4, 8, 32, 34-6, 39, 42, 45
photograph 55, 90, 105-6
pitch 25-6, 31
poetry slams 25-6
portfolio 67, 75, 93
positive pedagogy 7, 11, 14-16, 125
predict/ion 36-8, 41-2, 50, 100, 114, 129
Prezi 102-5, 107
problem-solving 34, 74
prosody 15, 68, 76
punctuation 47, 53

questioning 8-9, 22-3, 26, 63, 90, 92, 115, 121

recitation 8, 22-4, 30
repetition 47, 50, 60, 65, 92, 95
respect 2, 13, 86, 110
rhyme 2, 6, 14, 20, 32, 34, 37-8, 41, 47, 50-2, 56-7, 63-4, 66, 69, 74, 78-9, 85, 89, 91-2, 94-5, 102, 110, 123, 125-6, 129-31, 133
rhyming couplets 40, 78, 95
rhythm 1, 15, 25, 32, 38, 41, 47, 50, 52, 56, 59, 65, 76, 89, 103, 113, 119, 123, 125-6, 129, 131
role play 27, 33
rote learning 8, 22-3
rule/s 26, 46-8, 51, 53, 71-3, 78, 98, 100-1, 123

scaffold 49-52, 99, 129
skipping 123, 130, 133
song 6, 9, 14, 63, 66, 69, 79, 89-90, 94, 102, 109-10, 112-13, 116, 118, 120, 130
sonnet 78, 100, 125
spelling 4, 32, 37-8, 42-3
spoken word 25, 102-3, 127

stanza 20, 26-7, 32, 37-40, 50-1, 56, 76-9, 103, 115-16, 119-20, 124-5, 130
structure 7, 15-16, 40-1, 47, 49-50, 57, 72, 76, 78, 80, 92, 99-100
sustainable development 2, 74, 86, 96
syllable/s 51, 54-5, 60, 76-8, 99

technology 98, 100-3, 107, 133
theme 2, 7-9, 11-14, 19-20, 22, 24, 27, 32, 46, 50, 52-3, 57, 60-1, 69, 75, 78, 93, 103-4, 119
title 40, 43-4, 56-7, 93, 117
topic 5, 9, 12, 14, 19, 21, 31, 39-40, 50, 52, 66-7, 73, 75, 77-8, 80-2, 84, 91, 93, 100, 120-2
transform 7, 9-11, 16, 25, 33, 39, 45, 64, 84-6, 96-8, 104, 107, 110-11
translate/translation 39, 60-1, 63, 66, 68, 85, 99
truth 2, 72

universal 32, 53, 58, 64-5, 72-3, 78
utility, 69-71, 82, 128

verse 1, 10, 14
version 14, 20, 28, 31-2, 38, 41, 44, 54-6, 64, 66, 79, 99, 103, 114, 117, 131
vocabulary 13, 16, 18, 20, 22, 34, 40-1, 43-4, 48, 51-2, 56-7, 59-62, 67-8, 75, 81, 85, 89-92, 103, 110, 114-15, 118, 120, 125-6, 128, 132
voice 2, 6-7, 11-12, 14, 17-18, 20-2, 25, 27-30, 48-50, 52, 57, 65, 87, 94-5, 99, 103-4, 108, 111, 114-15, 122, 128-30
volume 25-6, 31, 115

For Product Safety Concerns and Information please contact our EU
representative GPSR@taylorandfrancis.com
Taylor & Francis Verlag GmbH, Kaufingerstraße 24, 80331 München, Germany